C000179175

"Being a parent to two beaut:
marriage, divorced and happily i
two, Karalee's book gives us appreciation of being a step
parent with a positively win-win intent. Yet, it is still a journey
wrought with challenges. Thank you for lifting the lid on step-
parenting conversations for merged families."

**Dr Yvonne Sum CSP, author of 'Intentional Parenting',
Growth Strategist, Hyperdrive Coach**

"A roadmap every blended family should have...filled with
sensible advice and incredible wisdom to help us find the
highest ground on an often rocky trail. Kudos, Karalee!"

**Susan Kurz Snyder, J.D. and M.B.A Georgetown
University, B.S. Cornell University, Founder, Principal
and Senior Legal Recruiter at Greene-Levin-Snyder Legal
Search Group, New York**

"Before I embarked upon the step-parenting adventure, I
recall an elder male asking me, *'Why don't you try something
easier ... like front line Afghanistan?!'*

Nowadays, as a grandfather and a veteran of single and
step-parenting, I reflect that the practical wisdom in Karalee's
book would have been of vital benefit to me both in my earlier
days, and beyond.

As parents and carers, we say we want the best for our
children, but actions are where it counts. By not dealing with
our own issues first and foremost, we effectively load those
consequences onto our children and those in our care.

"In this book, through straight-talking and clear examples, Karalee provides readers with valuable insights that reinforce how it is not all about us – the adults, and my, how positive this change of perception can be! This clearer perspective will help preserve the wellbeing of all involved in step-parenting, and I heartily commend Karalee's pragmatic, polished advice."

Garry Sarre, Master Photographer III, Accredited Professional Photographer, WA Commercial Photographer of the Year 2015, Sponsor of annual 'Free Headshots Day' for unemployed and students

"A rare pragmatic, common sense approach to the often delicate balancing act of step parenting.

Karalee has bravely shared some of her own step parenting experiences, which I'm certain will resonate with and inspire the many parents of blended families in our community.

This book illustrates that if we approach step parenting through the lens of the love for and welfare of our children, we all benefit and grow emotionally."

Liza Harvey, Western Australian State Liberal Parliamentary Leader, MLA Member for Scarborough, proud and happy step parent, parent and grandmother

"As a long term friend of the author, *Step Parenting with Purpose* opens discussion and provides great tips on step parenting for all types of families in today's world."

Linda Reynolds

"In *Step Parenting with Purpose*, Karalee skilfully weaves her own personal experience with stories from friends, colleagues and family members to give you an easy to read, no nonsense, practical guide to step parenting, that'll be a constant source of help and support.

Step parenting can be an emotional minefield, but Karalee doesn't tip toe gently into the subject, she strides in and tells you like it is and what you need to do to make it work, especially for the children.

And that is what is at the heart of the book; it's everyone's responsibility to make sure the kids feel loved and safe, no matter what it is going on around them.

I wish *Step Parenting with Purpose* had been around when I was 12, it could have prevented a lot of pain, heartache and therapy sessions later on!"

Josh Langley, Award winning children's author and mental health advocate

"*Step Parenting with Purpose* is a good read for anyone involved in the step parenting sphere with some valuable tips and sensible advice,"

Simon Creek BA, LLB, AIFLAM, Executive Chairman, Special Counsel (Family Law) & Nationally Accredited Mediator. HHG Legal Group.

"Step Parenting with Purpose" offers a personal and practical perspective on the challenges and joys of step parenting. But this book is more than your typical survival guide. It is filled with heart, honest and personal stories and the message that step parenting is a powerful role in a child's life."

Michelle Mitchell- Parenting Author, Speaker, Educator

STEP PARENTING WITH PURPOSE

KARALEE KATSAMBANIS

VIVID
PUBLISHING

ISBN: 978-1-925952-80-3
Published by Vivid Publishing
A division of Fontaine Publishing Group
P.O. Box 948, Fremantle
Western Australia 6959
www.vividpublishing.com.au

A catalogue record for this
book is available from the
National Library of Australia

– Contents –

One day you will
tell your story
of how you've
overcome what
you're going
through now, and
it will become
part of someone
else's survival
guide.

− Foreword −

To my husband Peter, who has always believed in me and loves me unconditionally. To my children, Andrew, Angelica and Zoe, I hope I am always fair to you and allow you to follow your dreams.

To Nicola, Vanya and Yasmin, for being on the journey with me and reaffirming that this was a book that needed to be written.

To my mother, for giving me the ability to be myself, free from pressure or expectation. To my stepchildren: without you, this whole book idea would never have transpired! To Josh Langley and so many other friends who have been on at me for years to get this written and published.

And to Jaqui Lane, Donna Parker and The Book Adviser team — without you this would have remained in the laptop!

– Introduction –

People are always told to write about what they know.

If they do that, then they have a ninety nine per cent chance of being successful in getting an extremely useful message across to help others and make a worthwhile difference in people's lives.

So, after nearly 15 years of being a step-parent I want to pass on my tips and experience in order to help you find more harmony in your step-parenting family.

I want to speak for all the step-parents out there and reassure you that as a step-parent you are actually doing a good job. No, you are not a monster, but are doing the best you can, despite coming under fire from many sides.

Do you wish there was a step-parent handbook full of advice that actually works?

Do you want a really happy step-family with minimal stress?

Do you want someone to help you navigate the challenging situation of step-parenting successfully?

Well, I wished for a yes to all of the above, and because I could not find a book which really helped me, I've written one because it needed to be written.

Nobel and Pulitzer Prize-winning novelist Toni Morrison pretty much nails it.

"*If there is a book that you want to read, but it hasn't been written yet, you must be the one to write it.*"

And so here we are. This is my story — and this is my life.

There are no mind-boggling statistics, no irrelevant information and no case studies.

Real life examples are always more effective than a well-meaning expert or academic who has not been through what you are going through.

Whereas I have been there, done that and am still doing it!

A friend of mine sent me this quote, which pretty much sums up what gave me the courage to put pen to paper, "One day you will tell your story of how you've overcome what you're going through now, and it will become part of someone else's survival guide."

Let's face it, navigating the step-parenting minefield is not easy at the best of times. Just when you think you have nailed one situation, you get another curve ball out of left field.

You need immediate answers, strategies and solutions to step-parenting problems for everyone involved.

It is all about consistency, keeping it simple and accepting that it is not easy.

You cannot build a successful step-family overnight.

There will be small steps and, more often than not, a few steps forward, followed by a few steps back.

Other times it will be large leaps and you will feel like it's a breakthrough and you've won gold.

This book provides tips and tools for you to get your life and your family back on track.

I do not claim to have all the answers, but I have experienced many situations that have cropped up over the years, and I know what worked and what didn't.

The essential, underlying principle is caring and wanting the best for every member of the family.

This book's purpose is to help you. You have probably picked it up, or someone recommended it, because you are at the end of your tether — or just curious about what to do next.

The role of step-parent is actually now so common that it is just as important as being a parent — and sometimes even more so.

Becoming a step-parent can happen to anyone at any

time. If you are prepared to become a step-parent, this will save you unnecessary hassle and stress as you will know some of the key things to not only look out for but to address.

This book is for everyone involved in the whole step-parenting family dynamic, whether you are currently a step-parent, have been a step-parent, are about to become one, are a parent, grandparent, aunt, uncle or even someone who thinks it'll never happen to you.

Well, think again, because that was what I thought my whole life, and it could not have been further from how things turned out.

You can only find real peace and harmony in step-parenting if everyone takes a step back, a deep breath and remembers that you cannot change what you do not acknowledge.

There are no mistakes in life, only lessons. But until you learn the lessons, you will keep on making the same mistakes and things will never improve.

And so, if parents and step-parents cannot put a stop to their bitterness and the continual blaming and fighting resulting from separations and divorces, then nothing will or can change.

That step back is to realise that it is not about them anymore: it is about their children.

I believe that if the children of divorced or separated parents don't see good communications and workable routines within their own families, down the track the odds of them becoming step-parents themselves are pretty high.

And the answer is that if these children, who will be the next generation of parents and step-parents themselves, actually learn good behaviours rather than dysfunctional and destructive behaviours from the adults around them, then they will know how to behave towards their own children and perhaps future stepchildren.

However, they cannot possibly begin to do this if they do not see some good behaviours displayed by their own mum and dad as well as their step-parent.

If they are not treated properly, chances are they will replicate exactly what they are seeing and the cycle will not be broken.

A step-family is a real thing, continually changing. It is fair to say that you cannot really talk to a child as an adult until they are well past 18 and have a bit more experience and some reference points of their own.

If they have been used as emotional pawns for years as they shuttle between homes, knowing deep down they are the meat in the weekly sandwich, you cannot really expect them to escape unscathed.

I ask you all to remain open-minded, to try and look objectively at your own situation and then, no matter what your age is, you may gain something from this book.

Everything in this book is based on real life experiences, not just mine, but stories told to me by many different people over the years. Mums in parks, people in supermarket queues, dinner party conversations, hair-dressing appointments, school pick-ups and drop-offs and anyone else you can think of.

It is amazing who tells you what, when and where!

"A good step-parent can literally turn the life of a child around."

"A child cannot have too many people who love them and want to help them succeed."

"A step-parent is so much more than just a parent: they made the choice to love when they didn't have to."

There you have it — three unknown people who said completely true things designed to make everyone just stop and think for a moment when assessing their own domestic situation.

You are just 15 chapters away from completely revolutionising your life as a step-parent — and knowing you are not alone in the journey.

Read on, enjoy, and above all learn, so we can have a generation of young people who know how to thrive, grow and become resilient.

– Prelude –

No one ever dreams of actually being a step-parent. It does not even make it onto a list of things people want to do in life.

We first learn about step-parents and step-families in fairy tales such as Cinderella.

No matter what, we all still want our own 'happily ever after', no matter how silly it may seem.

But when the Mr Right we meet has been a Mr Right for someone else before us and has children, it is a different kind of reality.

Your Mr Right may still be Prince Charming, but it can never be a simple case of boy meets girl.

So what do you do? Do you run as fast as you can from what could be the true love of your life simply to meet someone who ticks your list because they are single — yet could have a whole heap more issues in their life? Or do you realise that just because the love of your life has loved before and has children there may be a few molehills and mountains to climb, but they can be climbed as support is there.

And this is where I come in.

I have been in your shoes. I have faced the molehills and the mountains which will face you too, but because I have travelled this step-parenting road I decided to write this book because I felt there was nothing really relevant in the market to help me when I needed it and being able to share knowledge to help others is such a valuable and wonderful thing.

For some people, the rose-coloured glasses come off much sooner than others, but it does not mean it is always a downward spiral. Life ebbs and flows and so too does the step-family.

I want this book to help people, but also to give proper shout-out to all those step-parents who are doing the absolute best that they can, but who feel like they are dodging landmines between two warring parties. And for every landmine they dodge, there is almost guaranteed to be a grenade around the corner.

You are not alone.

At 33 years old, I originally thought I had it all. An absolute career woman at heart, vowing I would never get involved with anyone who had been married, let alone who had children from a previous marriage or relationship.

I was actually happily single, had loads of friends, enjoyed travel and the flexibility of doing what I wanted when I wanted. I had been a bridesmaid several times and attended many weddings, always delighted that my friends had found their 'other halves'.

I was considered a source of positive inspiration and optimism by all my friends. When asked, I was happy to advise them on their relationship woes as an objective, independent person. Everyone seems to have one friend who is single — that was me — while the others found someone or floated from one relationship to another.

And then Peter, now my husband, came into my life.

My life was so routine — organised into neat boxes — that I almost didn't go on our first date, because the idea of dating anyone with children made me run a mile in my head. Anyone in that category would have immediately been in the 'too hard box', never to be opened!

Like so many people, I had struck him out because he was divorced and had baggage — two children aged 11 and 12.

And then a friend of mine came out with an absolute pearler, which made me stop and think:

"Karalee, you are 33. Face it, the only men you are going to attract in your age bracket have either already been taken or are married or divorced. If they are single, there's a reason. Most likely they either don't want to commit or are happy being playboys and want their weekends with the boys. Otherwise you're going to date a man 10 years younger and end up being his mother! At least Peter has shown he can commit. You'll find out why it didn't work, but if you don't go out with him you'll never know. Oh yes, and watch how he talks about his ex and treats his kids. You learn a lot about someone from all that stuff," and with that she hung up.

She rang back.

"Karalee, something else I've thought of too. Think of the person, not the societal description he has been labelled with: 'divorced with two kids'. It's a date, not a marriage proposal and he is probably just as nervous, if not more so, than you."

Famous last words. From the first moment I saw him, I knew he was my Prince Charming.

And the rest as they say is history. We got married in 2007.

Those rose-coloured glasses have been wonky at times, but it is a matter of working things out in several paradigms and also realising that everyone wears those glasses in many situations, regardless of being a step-parent.

So I want to show you that before you put the whole step-parenting thing in the too-hard basket, after reading this book you will at least be in a position to make a more informed decision.

You may still decide that it is not a path you want to travel down and that is okay. But you may realise that a lot of the emotions you are feeling are completely normal when you embark on the whole step-parenting dynamic.

Being part of a step-family can happen to anyone and affect everyone. It is not an easy dynamic and sometimes external influences get in the way.

This book will save you a lot of unnecessary hassle and stress as you will know some of the key things to address and be mindful of.

All you can ever really control is what you say, how you say it and what you do.

Life does not come with a manual and a nice neat set of instructions, let alone when you are merging with someone else's life and the lives of their children.

I can help you not to make the common mistakes so many people do during separation or divorce. And, on the flip side, if you are already making those mistakes, how to stop and recalibrate your modus operandi and get back on track.

If I were asked to describe what being a step-parent was like, I would say just like the black jelly bean. Whether you love black aniseed or not, sooner or later you have to realise that there are black ones in every packet all around the world.

So, whether you are loved or liked or not as a step-parent, sooner or later everyone has to face up to reality and accept that, in the majority of cases, you are actually here to stay in a family that came along before you did.

Families nowadays are many and varied, but the essential principle of caring and wanting the best for every member of that family remains an underlying principle.

This book is not a cathartic experience enabling me to pour out my frustrations of 15 years of step-parenting, because I am actually very happy as a mother of three and step-mother of two. Naturally there are things I do differently with my own children that I would have liked to do with my stepchildren, but it all depends on the age stepchildren are when the newly blended family is formed.

You cannot alter the fact that your biological genes do not exist in your stepchildren, and sometimes they are just wired differently.

Step-parents are continually, like parents but perhaps more so, compromising, playing peacemaker and bending over backwards — far more than they would for their own children. That will always be part of the deal. It is just how it is.

More than often than not, step-parenting really is a thankless task and most step-parents who do the right thing are not appreciated. They are the ones who end up carrying the can, but are knocked by their partner's ex at every opportunity.

More games seem to be played by the partner's ex, instead of their accepting that the step-parent will be part of their child's life and asking how to make this work in the best way possible.

Yes, there have even been occasions when I have told my husband that his ex-wife is right — not that she would ever believe that!

You may even be waiting right now with dread and optimism for your stepchildren to arrive for a routine custody visit because maybe, just maybe, it has been a rough road with them for months, even years. Deep down you want the situation to change progress, but you are not quite sure where to begin.

This book can provide the tips and tools you need to be able to get your life back on track.

I do not claim to have all the answers, but what I do have is experience of so many situations that have cropped up over the years, and what worked and what did not — and hopefully this will help you.

I do not have a psychology degree, but what I do have is more than a decade of practical experience, an absolute passion for what I am writing about and an easy-to-read style that will help you when it comes to divorce and separation.

This book is designed to open your mind, provide different perspectives and get people to take responsibility for their own behaviour — and be able to look at the way they are behaving from the other side too.

Perhaps it can stop the damage being done to repeated generations of people affected by separation and divorce.

It is never too late for anyone to change their behaviour or how they conduct themselves, but it is important to remember that you cannot change what you do not acknowledge.

However once you do, your whole world will open up and become a better place.

– Chapter One –

THE SPLIT, THE SAVAGENESS AND THE SILLINESS!

The most uncommon thing is common sense.

And especially during a separation and divorce.

If you are in the process of separating or divorcing, flabbergasted at the cost of legal fees as well as financial settlement costs, then you probably have a friend who has been through it all and is trying to humour you by saying "you might as well find someone you hate and just give them a house — it's cheaper!"

That may make you smile, but going through a split is definitely not fun.

The end of a union is sad for everyone —the hard reality that a love story has ended.

When emotions are running high, common sense just goes out the window. Deep-seated anger that it hasn't worked is essentially what drives behaviour. The realisation that years have been wasted, and for what?

Sadly, revenge is sought in many different ways: financial, emotional, and very often using the kids for emotional blackmail, like when the father may see the children he not only fathered but has also seen every day until now.

None of this is helped by talk around the water cooler at work. We have all heard of someone who knows someone who used this lawyer or that lawyer, or is this what happened, and so on. Each situation is different and urban gossip simply clouds it all.

The jails are 95 per cent full of innocent criminals, right? Of course not, and when it comes to separation and divorce is it 95 per cent the other person's fault? Of course not. There are always two sides to a story, and the truth lies somewhere inbetween.

No matter what anyone says, you cannot undo what has been decided by either both parties, or the one who has initiated the split. It all has to play out through various phases with, hopefully, a workable resolution for all. But life is not ideal at the best of times, and the road to hell is inevitably paved with good intentions.

Suddenly, more often than not, it is the mother of the children who is now calling the shots and dictating when and for how long their dad can see them.

Throw in the fact that one or both parents has now met someone new and you have an explosive situation giving brinkmanship a whole new meaning!

Try to think outside this emotional triangle from a more objective viewpoint and perspective.

So what do you do when your world has been turned upside down and you can't see the wood for the trees?

You cannot undo what has been decided in terms of separation or divorce, but what you can do is realise that there is a new path ahead.

Hell hath no fury like a woman scorned. Whether your husband and you have decided it's the end of the road together, whether your husband has left you for someone else, whether you have left your husband for someone else, there are some things to keep in mind.

I can tell you what not to do — and deep down you know it already, but perhaps seeing it in print may strike a chord.

The first thing is, you don't bad-mouth your ex to your children ever! Even if he or she is more at fault for the split. No matter how tempting it is, don't. Children remember comments years and years later. Bite your tongue, ring a mate, scream and punch a pillow and call him or her every name under the sun when you are alone, but never bad-mouth your ex to your children.

If your ex has already moved on and met someone, and made the classic mistake of introducing their children to their new boyfriend or girlfriend, again, you don't bad-mouth the new partner to your children ever!

I think that too many people force meeting the kids onto their new partner far too quickly because they feel that they are being up front and honest and not hiding anything. But there is always a time and a place.

The problem with introducing the new partner too quickly is that it's confusing for the kids and, if your relationship doesn't work out, it can end up confusing for you too.

Of course, there may be exceptional circumstances.

Perhaps you are widowed or there is no way to wait to meet the children.

But, generally, the longer you wait the better it is for the children and, ultimately, the better it is for your new relationship.

It was nearly a year after I met my husband that I first met my stepchildren. That may surprise you, but friends said it was important not to complicate things and also to give the relationship a chance to develop.

The fact I worked many weekends gave him a chance to not only establish the new custody patterns of alternate weekends with his children, but also to go and see and support their sport on the weekends he didn't have them, and that worked out very well for us all.

Ultimately, you do indeed have to do what is right for you, but you should also keep your mind, eyes and ears open to advice from other people.

Not so that you become absolutely overloaded or worried about doing the wrong thing, but if you hear people say they met their partner's kids too soon and if they had their time over again they would have waited, don't automatically think that won't happen to you. Hear them out and see why it didn't work.

If someone is willing to open up to you and share their experiences, there could be some validity in what they say.

Or they may have simply been too immature to deal with the whole situation at that particular time.

Take it slowly and remember that if you are going through your split and you meet someone straightaway, you might be jumping out of the frying pan and into the fire.

There is nothing quite like the start of a new and exciting relationship to take your mind off present realities.

No one wants to dampen the butterflies in your tummy feeling, excitement and smiles, however you cannot go off skipping in the meadow with the daisies when children that you have created are involved.

Even though your mum and your dad are your mum and dad, they may not be as ecstatic as you are about this new potential relationship, because of the wisdom of their years and their life experience.

It is not to say they won't be happy that you have met and moved on with someone else, but it may take them several more months to adjust to the fact. Just be patient and give it time. They are worried about you, your children and life in general.

Just as your world has now changed, so has theirs. And step-parenting is all about being able to reach a good co-existing medium which works as well as possible for everyone.

While you are on the rollercoaster of new love, they are there waiting underneath in case it comes off the track — and they have known you for your whole life.

You do not need to reveal absolutely everything straightaway.

It will be nerve-racking for them, not to mention your new partner!

If you are the new partner who will be assuming the role of the prospective step-parent:

If you meet someone who has been separated for a couple of months and wants to introduce their children to you, unless they are widowed it really is too soon for everyone. Most importantly, it is too soon for the children.

The last thing they need is a revolving door of mum or dad's new partners coming into their lives.

They need time to adjust to their new world, and if you meet them too soon you will end up coming off second best as the kids will undoubtedly think you had something to do with their parents' breaking up.

Whether indeed you did have something to do with it is immaterial; this is the situation facing you now. Nice and slow is the real key.

Sisters, brothers, sisters-in-law, brothers-in-law, aunts, uncles, cousins of the people who are separating or divorcing:

This is for all of you out there who just cannot help

wanting to get involved — and you all know who you are!

Do you honestly think that the couple involved haven't thought about the impact of their actions in splitting up?

In fact, more often than not, they probably considered separating and divorcing several times before announcing it, and worrying about their parents, brothers or sisters' reactions is something they can do without.

If it is your son or daughter, brother or sister who is separating or is getting divorced, I have one crucial piece of advice for you:

No matter how close you are to them, the absolute best thing you can do is to butt out — and I really mean that.

Someone going through all this has already been bombarded with guilt, and it doesn't matter whether you saw them and their wife or husband once a week for lunch or dinner for years, you actually never know what goes on behind closed doors.

You may think you do, but you don't.

How many times have you been surprised when you learn that a couple you know, whom you thought were happy, suddenly splits up?

And how many couples whom you know niggle all the time, defy the odds and remain together?

What goes on in a marriage or partnership is between the two people involved and that's all.

Family is family and has its place, but that place is not now unless you can button your lip, be a true support, and not fan the flames. Telling someone now that you never liked their partner is neither helpful nor called for. They may in time get back together, and then how will you feel about having bad mouthed them?

Of course as an extended family member, the person's divorce will affect you. But their spilt is not actually about you.

Jumping in and saying things such as "what about the children?" is not helpful. It is downright stupid and insensitive.

The people separating or divorcing are going through enough emotional difficulties, and don't need to be hearing it all from well-meaning relatives or undergo a post mortem every time they meet someone.

Funnily enough, you may have seen more of your child or sibling precisely because you actually liked their husband or wife, who may have encouraged a close relationship.

You may have shared the same interests, gone on holiday together, taken your children to school together and all that sort of stuff. But now the ball game changes for better or for worse, and if you like your in-law better than your actual blood relative you will feel a real loss, but at the end of the day your loyalty really should be to your relation. This may be dreadfully difficult, but once the dust has well and truly settled, which may take months or years, you can maintain contact with the other person, especially if they are the godparent of your child.

Better still, just stay out of it and actually tell both

people you feel awkward and wish them all the best, but that you cannot be drawn into all this and they need time to process what they are going through, that you cannot be objective and perhaps they need to seek professional counselling.

Getting caught in the crossfire when it comes to family members is not fair on anyone, so just maintain that respectful distance and refrain from gossiping as it helps no-one.

Grandparents:
One of the really difficult areas to navigate is when it comes to the grandparents.

No one who is older than us ever wants to be told what to do, what they should do or how they should behave.

Helping them understand and be part of this new post-separation/divorce world can be more difficult than it looks, but it's possible if everyone is prepared to listen, take things on board and, perhaps more importantly, actually implement them.

Do not turn into the relative from hell. Keep a respectful distance and allow the dust to settle.

If your daughter is going through a break-up, she is your daughter and needs your support. Your son-in-law may have been the funniest person in the world and the best handyman around but, when it comes to something like this, your own adult child needs to know they can count on you. You do not have to be a stone wall to your son-in-law, but initially you must accept that he actually will not be your son-in-law much longer, although he will always be the father of your grandchildren. Your daughter needs to know that you are not going to be passing information to him until they reach an amicable settlement.

Another suggestion is, do not make phone calls saying "I can't believe my son/daughter has left you, you are the best thing that ever happened to them, etc..." It may help get things off your chest, but it does not help the person who is still grappling with hard cold facts in the light of day. And it does not help your own relative, who will find out in the end — although that may be one of the reasons for the call.

Everyone seems to want to get involved in stuff that does not really concern them, wants to have their say. It's human nature. It is unrealistic to expect relatives not to say something to the people involved, but there is a fine line – don't cross it.

There are always exceptions to the rules, and if you want to let someone know you are there for them you cannot be faulted — but there is a right way and a wrong way to go about doing it.

We are coming to the end of the golden generations of people who have been married for 50 years plus and struggling to understand the younger generations who, in their eyes, seem to split up as soon as the going gets tough.

Many people who have been married for more than 50 years might, many years ago, have liked the opportunity to leave their marriage. But in those days there was no government support for women and there were no no-fault divorces. Social stigma and being in the newspapers was not worth it for the women and children involved. A divorce completely destroyed a woman's reputation.

Not every golden marriage is truly golden.

If your child is breaking up, you will experience a whole gamut of emotions, but they are all normal.

You thought their life was settled and that your child was happily married, but now all that has been torn apart and you are uncertain about many things. This is not helped by well-meaning walking, tennis and bridge partners who chime in with second-hand stories of what might happen now.

If you listen to too many well-meaning social acquaintances it clouds your judgement. Everyone knows someone who knows someone — like the Chicken Licken story — who told them that the sky would fall in.

It won't. But your sky will undoubtedly turn from a sunny one to overcast until things sort themselves out.

Fear is a great motivator and it affects many people.

Fear will spur some people into grabbing the bull by the horns and trying to fix everything they possibly can.

Others people will say nothing and let internal worries take over.

The best thing you can do is to keep calm and take it one day at a time.

Sleeplessness nights will no doubt be the norm, as well as the maternal or paternal urge to protect your child who is now going through this painful process.

You will be saddened no matter whose decision it is.

Perhaps your next thought will be for your grandchildren.

You may be wondering if you will still be able to see them.

You may well be from the generation who always put a literal pen to paper and that is fine, but the person you write to may be surprised that you have contacted them. And you may not get the response you are after, regardless of how good your relationship was previously.

You may be livid if it is your son or daughter-in-law who has caused the split with your own child, no matter how old they are, but if you have grandchildren you need to rise above your primal feelings, use your head and not your heart, and work out how to see your grandchildren regularly.

Do you want to be one of those poor grandparents going through the courts trying to get access visits to their grandchildren? This is often what happens because in the beginning the grandparents refused to maintain a relationship with their daughter-in-law who traditionally ends up with the custody of their grandchildren.

Once the divorce is over, if you still have the wedding pictures all over your home you can re-live happy memories, but if your child is divorced and has met someone else, save yourself added agony and stress and take the pictures down.

Yes, it is your home, and by rights you should be able to do what you damn well like. But I am just trying to save you from age-old mistakes that people do not want to acknowledge, recognise or learn from.

Sometimes you have just got to be the bigger person, even if you do not want to be and do not agree with what has been said.

It is time to take the pictures down.

I can see you shaking your head and saying "what would she know?" Well, just trust me on this.

If you have been married for many years, never had a cross word and always done everything together, this is going to be an extremely raw stage for you to get through.

Unfortunately life does not happen in nice neat boxes. I have wrestled with softening my advice regarding taking pictures down, but then I would be doing you an extreme disservice in practical advice — and the whole premise of the book is to save you as much hassle as possible.

Take them down. I do not care how beautiful the day was or whether you still cannot believe the marriage is over or whose fault it was. Put them away in a cupboard or a drawer. You do not need to smash them and put them in a bin, just put them away.

Take them down.

Just think how you would feel if it were your son or daughter who went into their new parents-in-laws' home and there were pictures still up of the first wife or husband!

Are you now, excuse the pun, getting the picture?

You would feel for your son or daughter, wouldn't you? And realise that out of respect they would not ask them to take down the picture. Even if they asked their new husband or wife to have a word with their parents about taking down those pictures, it could take up to a year or more to happen.

So, as the parent-in-law (indeed, more often than not, you will also be the grandparent), why don't you make it easier for the new relationship to become established?. Even if you do not like your son or daughter's new husband or wife and find yourself always comparing and contrasting them to your first son or daughter-in-law, remember, this new partner will more often than not hold the key to your future relationships with them and the family.

Believe it or not, a small gesture will go a long way.

It will take an incredibly level-headed, mature person not to write you off if you do not take down constant reminders of the past — and there are not many of us incredibly level-headed mature people around when it comes to the initial stages of the new relationship and meeting the partner's parent(s).

So, win yourself an instant brownie point. Believe me, there will be plenty of other challenges down the track and the more you conquer at the beginning the better!

Your new son or daughter-in-law will always feel a little intimidated being the second husband or wife, but they cannot make up for husband or wife number one's shortcomings. They also cannot change how they are, but what they are is what has made your son or daughter smile, laugh and love once more.

And, if you are not ready to display a picture of your second-time-married son or daughter, there are other options.

Perhaps you have your reasons. You may wonder what your grandchildren will think if that original photograph is taken down but, believe me, everyone gets over it and if it does bother the grandchildren, they will ask Nanna or Poppa where the picture is and you will have time to find the right words.

I would suggest that a different picture of the first married couple, perhaps with their children, could be displayed if the grandchildren are fretting a bit. But not the wedding picture.

My husband suggests that another photograph be taken with the kids, and forget about keeping a picture with the ex in it.

He says that it is not only the feelings of the new spouse that are important. You don't want to visit mum or dad's place and see a picture of yourself with your ex.

You don't need a constant reminder.

I am not suggesting at all that you remove all reminders of the first marriage, but use some common sense and tactfulness.

And I urge the couple who have split up not to forget the golden oldies.

Yes, they may seem fuddy-duddy in their ways, but they have lived a lot longer than the rest of us and seen many changes. If they still hark back to the 'good old days', they have done their best for their children and are so often nowadays left to raise another family — their grandchildren — when their own children's lives have fallen apart through drugs and alcohol, something that hardly existed when they were growing up.

Do not ever rip up photos of the family. Your ex-son-in-law or daughter-in-law will always be your grandchild's father or mother.

Please remember this, and please remember that all the examples in this book are true.

You do have a right to be angry when you think of what you have done for that ex-son or ex- daughter-in-law, but, don't do anything counter-productive that won't help in the future.

Divorce and separation aside, we have all invested time in a myriad of relationships . If we kept score of absolutely everything we have done, then none of us would ever do anything for anyone.

I am sure if you helped the ex-son or daughter-in-law financially then your anger will be rising but, rightly or wrongly, that is life. Most human beings I know like helping people, especially their family, out and many people benefit indirectly as well.

You have every right to wish you had never bothered or want the money back, but in reality you know that unless you had a legal agreement drawn up then you have very little chance of success.

That utility bill or mobile phone bill you paid is paid. What are you going to do? Launch a court action for a few thousand dollars to try and recoup a few hundred dollars? Of course not. And at the time you paid it you were happy to, otherwise you would not have.

You win some, you lose some. All you can do in life is your very best at the time. Swings and roundabouts tend to even everything out.

Years later you will regret it if you defaced or smashed those framed photographs, and your grandchildren will remember.

It is not your role or perhaps even your right to destroy photograph albums.

What kind of a message does it send to your grand-children? Do you honestly want them to behave like that?

Actions like this have a lasting effect, and leave everyone speechless years later.

No matter how angry you may be, what is done is done.

It is now about moving on and having a workable relationship with all parties.

You may think your child is making the biggest mistake of their lives by breaking up with their spouse, but there are only ever two people in a marriage and only they know what goes on behind closed doors.

Remember, this book is all about looking at your own actions and encouraging the current generation to learn the right way to behave.

Wait a while, a few weeks at least — give it time. The couple who are splitting up do not want to rehash it over and over and over again with everyone they know.

When you hear someone has separated or is getting divorced, you know it is sad and private. That is a fact. It is the end of the union. No one goes into a union thinking it is not going to work, and you do not need to know all the intricate details of who said what to whom.

You have to realise that your gesture may or may not be acknowledged.

Your gesture may be in the form of a text, a written note or a voice message. If it is not acknowledged immediately, that does not give you automatic carte blanche to condemn the person and say "I texted or left a message or wrote a card and they didn't even say thanks."

You know deep down that they have received your communication and that they may need time to process what is happening to them and to their family, or simply may not want to talk to you. Try not to take it personally.

They will appreciate the fact you have reached out to them, but it may simply be a case of not knowing what to say to you. And they may well be embarrassed.

It may be years before your communication is acknowledged.

A high flying couple whom I was related to, who lived overseas and whom I had known from when they first met, decided to divorce after 25 years. They had two children. I sent a separate email to each of them because, while I had far more in common with the woman, I did not want the man to think her side of the family felt he was an enemy or monster. It was a lovely email saying exactly that and wishing him all the best.

Was I surprised he did not email back? Absolutely.

Had I put myself in his shoes and thought how good that her cousin has reached out to me and said these nice things? I thought I had, but I had thought about it from my own perspective, not his.

Four years later on an overseas trip, we met up with him and his children. I couldn't help but ask whether he had received my email as I had never had a reply. He told me he had really appreciated it, but even though he was someone who worked in communications he was too stunned to know exactly what to write in reply.

I said "maybe just thank you?"

"That's more difficult than you think, but I did get it and have kept it," he replied And he showed it to me.

I learned then that not everyone acts in the way you

might and nor how you might want them to act or as quickly, but that I had done the correct thing to let him know that, as sad as divorce is, it happens and does not erase all the good times.

This split is not about you so do not get offended if the response you expect is not what you hoped for.

We all wonder how we would act in a given situation, but until it actually occurs we really do not know.

Now some words of advice for the second spouse:
You are stepping into this family and fulfilling the role of a step-parent.

Yes, you may well be a lovely person, but do not be naïve. You will probably have to work overtime to gain the respect and liking of your new family — welcome to the world of second marriages. None of this is going to happen overnight. All you can ever do is be in control of what you say, how you say it and what you do day in and day out. You may have the very best of intentions, but sometimes things will go to custard as you cannot control everything. Stay consistent and take it one day at a time. Everyone will be just as curious about you as you are about them. That's normal.

Even if your new in-laws hated their son or daughter's spouse, the history is there — probably spanning several years — and they will still be trying to look at the positives even though it is now apparent the negatives have outweighed them. They do not want to think they wasted their time, money and emotions on someone who is about to leave or has indeed left their family.

Don't panic. Don't stress out. It is not always like this, but you have to just be you and realise that your in-laws will need some time. Their world as they knew it has now changed forever.

However, more often than not they will come around.

It is unrealistic to expect them not to have some contact with their ex-son or daughter-in-law if there are grandchildren involved.

Show that it does not bother you, even if it does — which it really should not. Be the grown up and do not make a fuss.

If your stepchildren are lucky enough to have grand-parents, you should never stand in the way of their relationship with them.

Most grandparents just want to continue to be in their grandchildren's lives and play a positive role in their future. Grandparents do different things from parents and step-parents and seem to have more patience and success in achieving what eludes many of us, from getting them to eat broccoli to doing their homework!

You cannot control what the grandparents may say about you, but hopefully their years of child raising, maturity and wisdom will prevent them playing you off against anyone.

All you can do is lead by example.

You may rue the fact your husband, wife or partner has

to pay child support, but what if you have children and your marriage breaks down? Seeing the conduct of your present partner in these circumstances speaks volumes, because if you end up their ex, you want them to do the right thing by you and pay child support.

Do not be naïve and say "Oh it'll never happen to us. We'll never split up. We're soulmates, etc." The people who walk down the aisle every year do not think they will get divorced, but some do and you may one day.

Your world may be turned upside down at any time. Years down the track, it may be your own adult children who separate and divorce, and perhaps you will play the role of parent-in-law.

Suddenly you will see things from a different perspective, in which case I hope this book will ground you and give you the tips and tools you need for a workable situation rather than an unresolvable stalemate.

This book is designed to help you think outside the square and adopt a calmer, more matter-of-fact, objective viewpoint and perspective so you do not act in a hot-headed irrational state of mind.

— Chapter Two —

THE END OF ONE ERA AND THE START OF A NEW ONE

If and when your ex-partner remarries, the build-up to the big day will evoke many feelings, some more valid than others, and it is important to be aware of them.

I cannot tell you how you should feel or what you should do. Deep down you already know, but knowing and accepting are two completely different things. I can tell you what not to do and how to save yourself frustration and regret.

Firstly, no one expects you to wave a huge banner and say "Yippee, I am so happy for my ex-husband" (or ex-wife). Nor to drown your sorrows in a bottle of vodka looking at your watch and waiting for the clock to strike as they say "I do". Nor do they expect you to stuff your face with chocolate cake, sit on the couch and not move for days.

This is real life. You will have mixed feelings on the day of your ex's wedding.

Those mixed feelings may range from good riddance, they are someone else's problem now, to I wish it was still me; why couldn't we work things out?

Relief and regret can be experienced simultaneously.

No matter how acrimonious your divorce, once upon a time, just like in a fairy tale, it was actually you getting ready to walk down the aisle with this person. You actually did, and thought you would live happily ever after.

Sadly, that did not happen, but it may down the track.

You do not need to mirror your ex's life and do everything at the same time. It is not a competition. Recover, recuperate and rebuild your life, so you can move forward as the years roll by.

Everyone involved in this new family dynamic needs to acknowledge and realise that things cannot ever be as they were, and this will be a period of huge change for everyone.

Time does not heal all wounds. You simply learn with the passage of time to live with things. But acting in anger — doing anything in anger — will merely backfire later in life.

The parent

Perhaps it is time for a new strategy or tool such as writing a journal or even a letter about how you actually feel.

Do not brainwash your children about your ex-partner's new fiancé or fiancée. It really will be self-defeating at some stage.

If your son or daughter has been invited to be part of the wedding party, do not automatically veto it. Instead, think how decent of their new step-parent to invite them.

If the step-parent wants to include your children, it is actually a good thing. Try not to convince yourself there is an ulterior motive. Nine times out of 10, it is not to one up you at all. Nine times out of 10, it is because the step-parent can see the bigger picture that you are still struggling with because you are still trying to process — and perhaps always will be trying to process — the fact that the union has ended.

I want to include three examples of what not to do if you feel your anger or jealousy are beginning to take over your everyday thoughts as the day your ex will marry again draws closer.

They are at the extreme end of behaviour, but nevertheless they have happened. Perhaps reading them in print will have an effect on you.

Please do not cut your daughter's hair on purpose if you know that rehearsals have been done with long hair for the role of flower girl or bridesmaid.

Please do not burn her bridesmaid's dress on purpose. The burnt soleplate print of the iron on the dress will be the talking point of the whole day. And you will be the one who ends up looking wicked. And deserve to.

However, ultimately, what is your daughter going to feel and remember? It is how the children feel on this day, not you. Little children do not understand the ins and outs of separation and divorce, nor should they. All they see is they get a chance to wear a pretty dress and shoes, hold some flowers and throw petals.

Do you really want to make a point by using your child as a pawn in a silly game? I hope not.

Please don't drop them off late at your ex-partner's or at the church. If jealousy is getting the better of you, delegate taking your children to a friend. You may hope to ruin their wedding day, but you will end up ruining it for your children and looking like a fool.

Just remember this: your time to get married again may be just around the corner and would you want your ex-partner to play these destructive games with you?

Ordering your children, or being Machiavellian in guiding them, to be as difficult as possible on the day and to scowl at your ex-partner's new partner yet smile like a cherub on cue is devilish behaviour — destructive, plain wrong and not setting a good example. Grow up and get a grip.

Marriage is a lottery, sometimes you win first prize on your first go and hang onto it forever; other times the first prize is completely wasted, but you still believe in the premise and want to try again with a new set of numbers.

Your ex-partner will have sat down with the children — and fiancée — and explained that nothing will change once they get married. They will still be the child's parent and see them and share in their lives and activities.

Every couple has their own way of doing it. All you can control is what you say, how you say it, when you say it, where you say it, why you say it and whom you say it to. You simply cannot control what the other party may or may not say.

Be the bigger person.

Always be the better person.

The behaviour of my husband's ex-wife in their divorce prevented her son and daughter from nearly being bridesmaid and groomsman at his sister's wedding six months before ours.

No matter how tempting it is, if you have not been officially invited (believe it or not, some exes do indeed invite their ex along with their partner to their wedding!), do not go anywhere near the church.

You turning up and being seen by a select few would probably ruin the day for your ex and his new partner as well as your children. Build a bridge, get over any feelings of resentment — which you will have as you are only human — and rise above it all.

You need to work out, work on and formulate strategies to avoid this.

That could be as simple as coffee or lunch with a friend, a personal training session, a swim, a massage — anything to avoid you doing something you'll regret later.

Hindsight is an amazing thing, but in this particular situation, you do not have that luxury and need to head off any irrational thoughts or actions.

You will have your chance to find happiness again if you want to in the future.

There are very few people who have not experienced a break-up. Break-ups, as painful and awful as they are, really do provide a chance to know who you are and allow your courage and resilience to surface — and realise that there will be light at the end of the tunnel. Until then, just being you is enough.

When you become the step-parent

Whether you like them or not, your partner's children will become part of your life and, as much as it might annoy you, you do indeed have to rise above the games, the tricks and the drama, to bend over backwards and make the effort to be as accommodating as you can.

This is new territory for everyone, but you are an adult and they are children caught up in an adult world. Their new world is now divided more often than not between two homes with two different conversations running through their minds all the time.

Be mindful of the fact that children are unable to comprehend all the ins and outs of life.

Your special day will not necessarily be theirs. That may be hurtful and hard to swallow, but it is true.

Whether they are five or 15, 20 or even 40 years old, nine times out of 10, children of divorced parents — no matter how much they may like you, think you are cool or do indeed get on with you — will wish it was their mum and dad getting married and not you.

Always try and include them in the arrangements. And be comfortable with the fact that they may be happy to come to the wedding but not want to be involved in any of the arrangements.

Of course, if their mother or father has died and you are essentially taking over the role of their only other parent, then it is another ball game and I think the importance of including them in all the arrangements is paramount.

Don't push or force them. Simply extending the opportunity to them, may make them happy.

When it came to our wedding, I invited my step-daughter and stepson to be in the wedding party, but I did say that they were either both in or both out of the bridal party.

I explained that if only one of them were a bridesmaid or groomsman, some of our 300 guests would ask why and whether I had asked them, and probably think I was a wicked stepmother for not including them both!

At ages 12 and 13, they both understood. My stepson had wanted to be one of his dad's groomsmen but he and his sister went away and thought about it. They were also each allowed to invite a friend.

Then they both decided to just come along and be part of the day and sit with their aunt and uncle, grandparents and the rest of the family.

My stepson did want to be a groomsman, and I like

to think that part of the reason for my stepdaughter not wanting to be a bridesmaid was due to "my mum would kill me", rather than "I don't like my stepmum." It was obvious that the brainwashing had included threats of "not getting things" if they were part of the day.

It's very sad when the children are used as emotional pawns in their parents' issues and want to please everyone without even really understanding what they are caught up in.

However, I did leave it flexible right up until the actual wedding day just in case they changed their minds at the last minute.

Sometimes while the decree nisi declaring the divorce is a legal reality, the financial settlement for both parties may not have officially gone through yet.

Very few separations or divorces are truly amicable. The years may elicit more compassion, but at the time it's emotional warfare.

If you are in the middle of getting the final financial settlement, a word of advice: your children should not be involved in this. It can create terrible anxiety for them, perhaps without you even realising. You need to compartmentalise all this.

It's no good saying your father this and your father that — or vice versa. These are adult issues. You need to find and talk about completely different interests and issues with your children, that don't revolve around your settlement.

Your marriage settlement is your business, not anyone else's. It should be between you and your ex.

Many people say that the only real winners are the lawyers. However, there is a need for objective advice, which is where they come in. Dragging it out for years and years does not allow you to move on and also drains your bank account.

Some people are consumed by revenge, instead of realising divorce mostly boils down to a formula, give or take a few percentage points. The sooner you can agree, the happier you will feel.

You need to realise that when you split up with someone, most of the time you are going to walk away with 50 per cent of what you had with them or slightly more or less.

I have never spoken to or met my husband's ex-wife. But I was always willing to for the sake of my stepchildren.

I certainly did not want a regular coffee meeting with her, but now as the mother of three children I know that were my husband and I ever to split up, and if he met someone else, I would be furious and upset but, having lived through one side of the spectrum, I would be mature enough to meet the new partner and lay on the line what I expected from them and listen to what they expected from me.

If you are the person whose partner has moved on, if they have met someone else, whether they marry them or not that person is going to have an influence on your child's life. If you rise above your anger and sadness, you will actually have a chance to find some common ground to work from.

I like to think that the majority of step-parents have more good in them than bad. There will always be some dreadful ones, just like there are always some dreadful parents. However, try and remember that the step-parent loves your ex-partner, which is undoubtedly hard to accept, and more often than not really does want to do the right thing by your children. They just need a chance.

There will always be people jealous that their partner has moved on and had more children with someone else. As a parent of three children myself, it is not about power or control, but if your ex-partner's new partner wants to meet you and does not have any children, then what is the problem? It is a confusing time for the children, so it is a chance to be able to lay down ground rules and iron out issues as well as being able to explain what you expect and how you would like things to work.

As a parent, you have to realise that your ex-partner's new partner is a real-living person who will play a part in your children's lives whether you like it or not.

It is immature not to go through with a meeting.

It can be in a neutral place.

It will be far more nerve-racking for them to meet the mother or father of their partner's children, especially if they do not have children themselves.

In my case, more than a decade has now passed and I have always believed that things turn out the way they are meant to. The road to hell is paved with good intentions and sometimes things have not gone the way I envisaged, however my conscience is clear. I have a good working relationship with my stepchildren and have shown them how to behave, never bad-mouthing their mother or her family and never trying to control them or be a mother to them. I hope and believe I have been a positive influence and that they look back and see I tried and continue to try my best.

Children will always have a loyalty to their mother and father, especially during a divorce, but do not underestimate how uncomfortable they may feel with their own parents' behaviour, especially if it is in stark contrast to a step-parent whom they know is trying their best.

If all a child hears is their mother criticising their stepmother and father, yet their stepmother never says anything bad about their own mother, they will wonder why.

I have always believed that you can only control what you say or do. You have absolutely no control over the other person.

Lead by example and be consistent so people see what you stand for and how your values shape your life.

Do not buy into the bitterness of the ex. It is the ex's problem.

If you are the ex, perhaps keeping a journal documenting how and why you feel things may be a good tool. To be able to reread it, look back and process how you got through a particular period may not only help you but also others caught in the crossfire.

This book has been called brave, brave because I have had the courage to actually say and outline what others sweep under the mat and hope to forget.

I am not a wishy-washy person. I am known for straight talking and not playing games, but although I am outspoken I do not get everything right.

Using examples from my own life within this book may give the impression that I want a cathartic experience.

That is not the case. However, if I do not include the examples to illustrate a point, then people will not believe what I am saying is true. Naturally any other side of a story would result in denial, but that is not my aim. I wish to make the reader stop, think and refrain from doing unnecessary, unhelpful things.

My husband's ex-wife came to our home open with a friend on a rare 40-degree day in Melbourne, and missed her daughter's netball final. That was her choice. There are always two sides to a story and she probably never told her friend she was missing the match.

Their names were in the agent's visitors' book, but the vulgar note I found later in a chest-of drawers was childish.

Instead of being angry, I felt sorry for her as I would not dream of doing that, let alone wanting to see a home years after the divorce.

Whether she knew that the house agent gave a list of all visitors to the home opens to us or not, she evidently signed it to get a rise out of my husband. We ignored it all.

People often say "Oh they will meet someone soon enough and all the emotional blackmail will stop."

What I have come to realise is that the emotional games and ridiculous behaviour of ex-partners can actually never stop until they admit the pattern of the behaviour.

It is the same with everything. You cannot change what you do not acknowledge, because you will simply keep on making the same mistakes.

Don't encourage friends to behave foolishly. Suggest counselling to learn to deal with the situation.

Counselling may never fix the hurt, but it should make you realise that hurt feelings are normal and begin to move on.

As I said earlier, children whose parents are separated or divorced will be part of the next generation of parents and step-parents.

They learn through example and it is our duty to rise above our anger and disappointment at the failure of our own relationships and show a different way to behave.

Learning how to behave differently does not mean all is forgiven, but it provides a more workable solution and strengthens the new dynamic of the step-family.

Ultimately, the biggest impact of your behaviour is on your children.

Maintaining those boundaries between adult problems and children is crucial. You need to protect your children as much as possible from all the emotional conflict going on between you and your ex.

Burdening them with adult problems is not the way to go. Children do not have the coping skills or the emotional maturity to understand money worries, adult relationship issues or their parents' unhappiness.

I cannot emphasise enough that parents really need to make their co-parenting a workable, conflict free zone because emotional scars on children can last a lifetime. I know many people in their 40s and 50s who are still wrestling with the impact of their parents' divorce and subsequent actions on them.

If all parents can try and work together rather than against each other, and keep the interests of the children at the forefront of all decisions, then things may start improving and getting better.

You are always responsible for your own words and actions. You cannot control what others will say or misguidedly believe about you.

Chapter Three

THE REALISATION THAT YOU ARE ABOUT TO BECOME A STEP-PARENT!

No bones about it, becoming a step-parent is a daunting prospect. Responsibility can overwhelm you, along with feelings of self- doubt. Completely normal!

But it can be rewarding. It may take a few years, perhaps decades, but your contribution will be appreciated at some stage, by your partner, the children themselves, and perhaps even the exes and extended family.

However more often than not, bitterness between exes overshadows your effectiveness as step-parent.

Whether you are an ex, a new step-parent or a child, watch the 1998 movie *Stepmom*, starring Susan Sarandon, Julia Roberts and Ed Harris. It is as valid today as it was then — a classic of what not to do as an ex and a new step-parent.

From the very beginning I was called KT by my step-children (my first initial and the initial of my maiden name) and still am.

A few years ago a friend of mine, Jane (not her real name), who is at the top of the legal fraternity and knew I was writing this book, asked for advice. She and her husband John had split up when their son Robert was five years old. John had had an affair with another lawyer at the firm where they both worked. He had subsequently married her and was insisting that Robert call her mummy too. This did not sit well with my friend as Robert was getting really confused.

I told Jane that as she was now with a lovely man, Harold, she should tell her ex-husband she was perfectly happy with that, and that Robert would now call Harold daddy too so he could have two daddies.

Needless to say, the two mummies were never mentioned again and Robert calls his stepmother by her first name.

Jane was astounded she had never thought of this solution, but I explained that it was because I was an outsider looking in, whereas she was wound up and governed by emotion and just could not see clearly.

That is what friends are for. Sharing knowledge. Helping to find honest, real solutions.

Time and time again, friends who were marrying and becoming step-parents were simply amazed that the basics of parenting had not been instilled in children — from hygiene to homework, moodiness to manners: simply general behaviour.

As we shared stories, we realised that there was indeed a common link and there are times when enough is enough. Yet it always seems to be the step-parent who has to see sense and remain objective. You can pick your friends but not your family — and you can relate to similar values and behaviours.

Ex-husbands and wives still angry over the breakdown of their relationship use their ex's new partners as emotional punching bags too often — and encourage their children not to respect them.

This is not on.

Treat other people as you would like to be treated. It is not rocket science!

You are both parents, and equal respect and love should be shown.

You may not be united in terms of being a married couple any more, but you need to be as parents, allowing your offspring to see that there is a right way of behaving and a wrong way.

You cannot command respect if you are not respectful towards others.

The message for all parents is, if your children are lucky enough to have a step-parent who actually wants to be part of their life and do things for and with them, be bloody grateful and stop the schoolyard antics.

So your ex has left you or you have left your ex. They cheated on you, you cheated on them, and so it goes on.

It is sad, but it has been happening since day dot. There are no guarantees, except death and taxes — you just have to be practical.

You have every right to be upset and angry, however you cannot change what happened and how your relationship ended. What you can change is how you deal with it and how it affects your child.

"It is not the set of cards you are dealt in life, it is how you play the set of cards you are dealt." That's a good saying — and always valid.

Surely, the ex can put themselves in the step-parent's role, stop and think how they would like it if they became a step-parent and were being treated like that by their new partner's children?

If the ex cannot do that, then they need to learn.

What so often should be common sense for adults, simply is not. Indeed, just because you are an adult does not give you emotional maturity.

We are responsible for our own actions. We choose how to behave. Sometimes we get it wrong and sometimes we get it right. As long as we are continually learning and sharing the knowledge with others we create a pathway for successful step-parenting.

The power of an apology cannot be underestimated. It is never too late to say sorry, whether for how you behaved towards your ex, or just how the whole situation unfolded. This is not a blame game; it is about the inner strength to acknowledge things.

It may take years, decades — and it may never happen. You do not need to apologise, but you may feel that it could release the dead weight you have been carrying around.

I cannot tell you what to do, but if wanting to do something like this has been on your mind for years, have the confidence to just do it! Being proactive with mental health is very important for everyone involved in a step-parenting situation.

We live at a time when TV shows such as *Oprah* and *Dr Phil* have opened the box on talking about social issues. Divorce and separation do's and don'ts are nothing new, yet the very fact that your ex-partner is now with someone else seems to cloud any reasonable judgement you ever had.

Your ex may have moved on, and it may take you several years to have another relationship, but Murphy's Law ensures that, even if you are a parent already, becoming a step-parent is a completely different ball game.

Imagine someone who has never had children suddenly finding themselves as a step-parent.

Sometimes the step-parent is stricter and tougher with their own children than their stepchildren, because they do not want to be accused of being unfair.

In the beginning, I wondered if my husband's ex-wife ever asked herself what it was like for me when I first met her children, but I was jolted back to reality by knowing that she would not have given it a thought.

Once I did all the children's sports, uniform and holiday laundry and packed it in bags for them to take when their Dad dropped them back at the end of a holiday week. Ten minutes later, my husband got a screaming, ranting phone call along the lines of how dare that woman, covering a range of issues which had little to do with the stepmother doing a stack of washing and ironing to save the mother from being lumbered with it all at 5pm on a Sunday evening when there was school the following morning.

So for the next few years I did no washing or ironing on weekend visits. I believe she later regretted this. However, let me be completely clear that the children's clothes kept at our house were always immaculately washed along with sheets, towels and everything else!

An early conversation face-to-face or an email regarding expectations on both sides could have saved all this unnecessary angst.

See, this is what I mean, most step-parents have good intentions and want to help, and when that is thrown back in their face it is not good.

No one was able to give me a manual to deal with stepping into the role of stepmother.

I had to use my common sense, read a lot of related articles, many of which were not particularly helpful at the time, and then make up my own mind whether what I was doing was working or not.

When I came into her children's life I should have

been able to meet her on neutral ground, primarily to find out what she expected of me and to be able to assure her that I certainly didn't want to take over her role of mother to her children, but I also needed to know that we had similar thoughts on parenting. And if we didn't, then how would we resolve things.

At this stage I had no children of my own, but was well aware that expert advice and the day-to-day reality of child rearing are two completely different things.

I think for anyone going through a separation or divorce it really is important to meet, even through gritted teeth, and work out some rules and routines.

For example, if the step-parent expects children to do small chores like making their bed, hanging up a towel after a bath or shower, putting dirty clothes in the laundry hamper, yet their own parent does not make them do anything like that at home, it does not do anyone any favours in the long run.

My own stepchildren were pretty good. Towels on the bathroom floor needed to be picked up. After I had done that several times, I merely left them there one morning — the floor was always hygienically clean — and when it was time for their evening shower, nothing needed to be said.

They had both worked it out and it rarely happened again.

My stepdaughter has told people that she respects me and remembers that when she was younger I was always firm, but fair and consistent — and more importantly if I said no to something, I actually explained why. That was more important to her than anything.

Going into the city by herself on a train to a concert or to meet friends was not allowed, because while she regularly caught the train with her school or with us, going alone as a young girl was not safe. She said that her mother would not explain why and just said no.

I told her that it was not we did not trust her to go to the concert, but that strange people lurked in the specific area she wanted to go to, who could pick up on naivety and young girls, and nasty things could happen such as kidnapping. And then she added "or murder".

I was not even thinking murder, but was relieved she said that as opposed to rape.

Children are not silly, and if you take the time to explain things to them it goes a long way.

I was not expecting them to be perfect. No one is. But I thought that part of the whole parenting caper was to get your children ready to function in the world. Very few people have servants or people to pick up after them the whole time. And what if my stepchildren were invited to a sleepover at one of their friend's houses,?

One can only try, and one can only do one's best.

They each had their own set of sheets and bedding at our house, and we let them choose their own doona covers and pillow case. If that felt more reassuring to them, which I have learned down the track it did, no problem.

One of my friends had an ongoing battle with her stepchildren and husband regarding bedding.

Your beautiful crisp, white 1000 count Egyptian sheets, with matching pillow cases, bolsters, doona cover, throw rug and several scatter cushions tying in with the room's decor which you envisioned for your guest room 'ain't gonna' happen with stepchildren between the ages of 1-18!

My friend kept telling me that her stepchildren's bedding was not her taste and did not match the house. I told her, it would not be like that forever and to just go with the flow. And that unless she was being made to sleep in the fluorescent configurations of various sheet and doona sets, who cared!

She insisted that it was her house and I agreed, but pointed out this was a stepfamily situation and sometimes you just have to give in and realise that whether it is one week on, one week off or every alternate fortnight, it is the stepchild's space and allowing them to make a contribution with their flair and expression is just another way to get more harmony in your day.

A wonderful friend of mine summed it up perfectly: "Close the door and write off 10sqm for the next 10 years! Pick your battle!"

No one is going to judge you if they come over and see mismatched bedding alongside exquisite decor in the rest of the house.

It seems like such a silly thing, but it ties into the whole dynamic of how the step-parent can often feel that they are unimportant and everything revolves around their stepchildren when it is their house.

This is just the way it is sometimes. But if you can break it down and try to focus on the bigger picture, you will get that harmony.

Step-parenting is a lot of give and take. It just is. It has to be, otherwise it all falls in a heap. But make sure you focus on really important areas — which doona covers and bedding are not.

The real key to this whole situation is to make step-children feel welcome and important in your lives.

All children learn how to play off one parent or adult figure against the other, and they pick up on any underlying tension between a parent and step-parent.'

That is why you need a united front.

Perhaps there should be a handover book or a diary, which could be used as a strategy if you are not on speaking terms with your ex, to outline what is needed for each visit. For example, there may be an orthodontist appointment after school or a weekend birthday party.

It is also a way of ensuring that no one forgets or miscommunicates and shows the children responsibility and how everyone needs to play their part in the new dynamic.

There is no temptation to write sarcastic comments in a handover book with all medical details and important phone numbers in the front as you know the children will see it.

In the beginning, I made excuse after excuse for my husband's ex-wife. She had got married and had her children in her early 20s, she had had a dysfunctional family dynamic growing up and merely replicated aspects of it — then one day I simply thought enough is enough.

We have all had problems. From my point of view she was not looking at the situation with any objectivity, and there comes a time when you cannot keep blaming someone else and expect to get bailed out.

Everyone is ultimately responsible for their own behaviour, and we all know that when you choose your behaviour, you choose your consequences.

The job of any parent is to prepare their child every day to function as an adult and make a valuable contribution to their community and the world.

It is not fair to do absolutely everything for your child or they will not have the chance to experience what you have experienced and that is how you grow, mature and develop as a person.

It is also unrealistic to think that for two to three days a fortnight you can parent them if the parent they are with most of the time does not back you up. It is the same if the step-parent contradicts everything and does the complete opposite from the main custodial parent.

If you know a party is coming up and the child's mother does not want them to go, do not try and be the cool father or step-parent and let them go.

There is a reason for everything.

Parents are not there to be their children's best friend, nor to be classed as the favourite parent either.

And if you should be in that situation one day, I guarantee you will not appreciate someone going against your wishes.

Chapter Four

SURVIVING THE FORTNIGHTLY ACCESS VISIT!

Tips for turning a sometimes hell into a sometimes heaven!

If you are now a step-parent, grasp the following two tips and move forward with gusto —and never doubt yourself or tie yourself up in knots again!

Biggest tip #1: Get over the fact your partner has indeed had sex with someone else and created a child or children. That was in the past, which is why he is now with you!

Biggest tip #2: It is perfectly ok to wish that your step-children were not around all the time, but they probably wish you were not always around too! There are times you will want to lock them in a cupboard and feed them stale bread and water, but everyone clashes in step-parenting at one time or another. As long as it is merely a jest, you're doing ok!

Remember Cinderella? We are all introduced to the stepfamily at a very early age. Do you want to be the wicked stepmother or stepfather or do you simply want to give this step-parenting thing a try?

We live in a complex world and while a quick Google will reveal a myriad of resources, blogs and chatter about parenting or step parenting, there are no actual rule books or manuals that reveal the golden key for how you can be the best parent or step-parent. All you can do is treat others as you would like to be treated and try your best.

Nothing automatically means that you will be treated kindly by your stepchildren, no matter how good you are to them, but they will soon work out whether you are a decent person, and even if they never apologise for past behaviour, they will know deep down if you have always tried to do the right thing.

When they went back to their mum, I would always say to my stepchildren "Have a lovely time with your mum and try to help her around the house. She is working full-time too, you know."

Remember, deep down children whose parents are divorced always want them to get back together again. In their minds, there is an idealised notion of how it was.

It is usual for them to cling to this, even years after their parents may both have remarried or repartnered. There is always a nostalgia for their parents to reunite.

Your partner's children from a previous union are not your whole life, but they are part of your life and your partner has to realise that whereas they may have focused on their children while they were trapped in a bad relationship and did not know how to get out, there has to be some adjustment now.

That adjustment, as I like to call it, does not suddenly mean abandoning the children and going out all the time with the new partner. Rather it means that the person needs to realise that if he or she cannot compartmentalise creating a new relationship as a couple and then adding their children to the mix, then they are not being fair to their new partner.

For example, if you are the parent who attends every single event your child is involved in, not just on your access weekend, but every single weekend, pretty soon your new partner may justifiably feel a little sidelined. You need to learn to share your time.

But this is very different to them being jealous of your relationship or time with the children. There is a reason why in the majority of cases custody is alternate weeks or weekends. It is to give the parent time off. If you have nothing except your children in your life, for your own sanity and the future, develop an interest or hobby.

It can be anything: the gym, playing sport, stamp collecting, birdwatching, wine and cheese appreciation, reading, the movies — absolutely anything, but make an effort to actually invest time in yourself, your life and your future.

Develop a routine to help it happen, and you will find your mojo naturally and then find yourself again.

You have heard of empty nesters who do not know

what to do with themselves when their children leave home. Each generation of children seems to grow up more quickly and, like you once did, they move on. They will not ring you as much as you want them too, and perhaps not even see you as much as you would like once a girlfriend or boyfriend comes along.

Your new partner needs to see that you can actually cope without your children 24/7, so that they can envisage a life with you. You must invest in this relationship too.

If you are moping about every alternate week or weekend that you do not have your children, it is not healthy for you, it is not healthy for the new partner and, if your children knew you were moping, it certainly would not be mentally healthy for them.

Missing them is only natural. Learning to actually create your new future is absolutely nothing to feel guilty about. But you have to pick yourself up, dust yourself off and start all over again — just as Frank Sinatra sang!

Whether you were married or not, there would be times where you would not see your children if a work assignment meant you had to leave early in the morning and come home late at night or were in a fly-in, fly-out (FIFO) situation for days or weeks at a time.

It is the same after dropping them back at your ex-partner's place. Naturally the quiet after a boisterous backseat of children will be eerie, and at the beginning you need something scheduled after the handover to try and take your mind off it.

Playing your favourite music as you drive home or ringing a friend hands-free for a chat is ideal. Then perhaps go for a walk or to the gym, take the dog for a walk, catch up with a couple of friends you haven't seen for a while or even sort through stuff you've meant to do for ages.

You have to realise that it is your new partner, not you, who is having more upheaval in their life by accepting the fact that you come with children. No matter how much they may love children, it is a huge thing which you are probably underestimating. Those children are now part of life.

There will be no spontaneous dinners, dates, weekends away — it will all revolve around the children's schedule, which is a big ask. However, your new partner will be happy to do it as long as they can see that you want a relationship with them and not just someone to share the parenting of your children, emotional support or financial support.

Just remember all that.

No matter how sure you may be that this new relationship will work, it is a very different ball game. And even if your new partner has children of their own, you will still expect time invested in you and your new relationship.

It does not matter what the experts say, the reality of a situation is always different.

In order to have a good relationship with my stepchildren, I had to work it out and read articles, dismiss some suggestions and become very objective. Some situations are painful, but you have to be confident that you are doing the right thing.

My husband was once told that kids work out what works for them, and it is true. However, if a parent is unhappy, they pick up on it. If they see their parent happy again with someone new, they may not initially like it, but they will notice how the parent's mood changes.

I always remember a friend of mine who was going through a divorce when I met my husband saying that while she was still really angry with her ex-husband and did not like his new partner at all, the crucial thing for her was that her ex-husband's new partner treated her children very nicely. That was all that mattered to her.

And all that should matter to you is that your ex's new partner is treating your children nicely.

You may think the word nicely is a little strange, but nicely is a vanilla word and I chose it because it is very unlikely that you will love your ex's new partner (sometimes it happens, but it is hardly the norm), but as long as the basics of feeding, watering, speaking to and acknowledging, showing interest in and smiling so as to establish a good relationship with them is done, it's nice.

A step-parent is going to be involved in the upbringing of your children, and you are the one who can make it a positive experience for them — if, and only if, you can just move beyond the bitterness of your relationship breaking down.

No one needs Einstein's brains to work out the basics. Comments from stepchildren, such as "How come you don't bad-mouth my mum/dad?" means that they are bad-mouthing you.

All that happens is that the children work it all out and suddenly become upset that their mum or dad is critical of their new step-parent, who may or may not be pretty cool in their eyes.

What should they do? Act like a spoilt brat? Or sit there churning internally over what to do, even though deep down they know what they should do? So they learn deceptive behaviour very early on.

Remember, children see things through a completely different prism from an adult.

They are busy enough — they don't need to expend energy on two different behaviours at two different homes!

My experience of deceptive behaviour in children is that once it is learned, it is quite a tough job to discard completely and may continue into late teens and early adulthood.

For example, I took my stepdaughter to see the Hannah Montana 2009 chick flick. She had wanted to go for ages, and the weekend it came out was her weekend at our place. If she had to wait for the following weekend at her mother's she would be 'so uncool' to her friends as they were seeing it this weekend!

So, off we went, chatting about lots of things to do with

school, sport, likes and dislikes, and she saw the movie, enjoyed it and all was well in her world.

Later on her mother rang her and I overheard her say "nothing much, stayed in, watched TV, homework, listened to my IPod."

I immediately thought how sad that was.

Why should she not have had the freedom to simply say "I went to a movie with KT," and her mum could have said "that's nice" and then moved on to the next topic.

If you have a chance to U-Tube a clip of *Mrs Brown's That's Nice* episodes, it will do you the absolute world of good. It is less than a couple of minutes, but really does put all this sort of stuff into perspective!

Like countless other children in her position, my step-daughter did not have that freedom, precisely because she knew her mother would go absolutely nuts.

The sad thing is that the mother would look on the stepmother taking her daughter to a movie as a bid to take over her role. Trust me, in 99 per cent of cases, no step-parent ever wants to do that and simply wishes the blackmailing would stop.

Straightforward objectiveness seems to go out of the window.

In a nutshell, to all parents, just be bloody glad the step-parent is even bothering with your child, whom you may not want to believe could behave in a way that would try the patience of a saint. But, trust me, the child does and will, regardless of age.

Instead, think to yourself "I may not like it; I may not even like them, but that's a nice thing they did for my child."

As a parent, have you got any of these insecurities? Have you acted like this? Be honest. It is not a failure to admit that you have acted like this or do harbour some unfortunate insecurities.

Is it really any different if your child's friend's mum takes them to the movies? Not really, so why make a big deal out of someone doing something nice for your son or daughter?

It is never too late to change or hold out the olive branch to try and build some kind of a working relationship for the good of your children.

Swallow your pride and grow up.

Put yourself in their position. Becoming a step-parent yourself is only ever a step away. Do not ever say it will never happen to you, or you will never remarry. Famous last words! You may have to eat them!

Treat people the way you would like to be treated, and your world will become a more bearable place.

No one is ever happy 100 per cent of the time, but if you start out from a negative mindset you will always be on the back foot.

If you have read this far, I may have actually touched a nerve and perhaps you can identify with what I have written?

Or perhaps you have never thought of step-parenting in this way, and its impact on your new partner, your children or your ex.

The bottom line is, as a step-parent you are never on holiday.

Your responsibilities are always there.

People will say but they are not your actual children, and while that is true, they are your partner's children and they are part of the package. When you made the commitment to be together, you knew all that.

In reality, though, the step-parent is the silent, unacknowledged sufferer in most new unions, who should usually win a gold medal for rising above what is being dished out!

While I am writing this book from an adult perspective, it is not rocket science to pick up on what my step-children have described as the weirdness of the whole situation when parents split.

How do children feel when their parents are going through a separation or a divorce?'

We will never ever know unless we remember.

It is well known that children often blame themselves for what has gone wrong in their parents' marriage, regardless of how many times the parents assure them that it is not their fault.

From my experience as a step-parent, getting your children into professional counselling is the number one thing, and it is often the child who says they do not need any counselling and is fine who will suffer in a few years or even decades.

Teenagers are challenging. You may have to resort to saying that if they do not come with you for counselling then they cannot go to camp, or use the car or whatever you think appropriate under the circumstances.

Too many people put too much responsibility on children aged 12 and over, and are so concerned about what the child wants that they forget at 12 years old you don't really know what you want yourself.

At least get them to a few sessions of counselling and get the counsellor's advice.

Even if that does not work for them, at least you have tried. But when they are 17 or 18, you can at least have some hope not to have to put up with dysfunctional behaviour stemming all the way back to the separation and divorce and now manifesting itself as they manoeuvre into young adulthood and want to form their own relationships.

But you may also need counselling, even if you feel fine and perhaps relieved that your marriage is over.

It is only a matter of time before a familiar situation will trigger something inside you.

It is not fair to yourself, your children or your next partner if you do not get professional help now so you can look forward to a brighter future and not be weighed down.

The reality is that no one is perfect, but there are ways of dealing with situations — and ways not to.

Life coaches are all over the place, and people go to see them for future direction, validation or whatever else they are searching for.

Going to see a counsellor is much the same.

Someone who can hopefully provide an objective point of view: look at the situation and navigate a way forward.

You do not need to tell anyone you are going to one if you don't want to.

It is perhaps better not to mention it. If your divorce has gone through but you are still in court thrashing out the financial settlement, leave the thrashing in the court-room.

As I mentioned earlier, your financial settlement has nothing to do with your children and they should not be involved in financial affairs.

They should not know who got what, etc. It is not their business.

The anger and resentment that stems from the financial settlement has little to do with the actual money involved; instead it is deep-seated emotional anger that the marriage has not worked and, more often than not, the fact that one person has already moved on with someone else is like a red rag to a bull.

That is what it all boils down to and really what all the anger is all about.

Be honest — even if your partner gave you the house, the cars, the boat, the poodle and the whole kit and caboodle, if you were describing to someone else what you actually ended up with, you would still say it was not fair and it was not enough.

You want them to suffer more than you, but this should not be at the expense of the child/parent relationship. This is not about being the winner or the loser. This is real life and you are living it.

So 99 times out of 100, you are unable to be objective because you have been rejected by someone you once fell in love with.

No-one likes rejection, ever.

You did not walk down the aisle imagining it would end like this.

But now is the time to realise that the little human beings you and your partner created are the important ones, not you, and you need to rise above it all and be the better person.

In the majority of cases, the greater amount of child support is paid by the man to his ex-wife.

Most non-custodial parents are required to pay some type of child support, and most Australian states have a set minimum amount that applies to even those who are disabled or unemployed.

You are paying child support because it is a parent's responsibility to financially support a child.

If you are one of the lucky people whose ex faithfully

pays the child support week in and week out, has the children at the agreed times throughout the year and does not abandon their children, then just button it and be thankful they have not turned their back on their responsibilities. There are countless examples of people who have.

Your ex should not have to pay for the crime of having moved on more quickly than you.

Regardless of the assessment, you will always think it is not enough. And that is a result of emotions and anger over the whole separation and divorce.

Plenty of people in your position do not receive the required child support.

And spending child support on your mortgage, rent, utilities does not cut it.

It is tough, but it is a chance to be a role model for your children.

The current economic climate in Australia, as in many other countries, is tough. And yes, sometimes the alcohol and the cigarettes have got to go. But that child support money is for children, and while you are required to look after them, you need to spend it on them regardless of your circumstances. You would have to pay the mortgage, rent and utilities no matter what. There may at times be exceptional circumstances where some child support money is needed to top up the rent or mortgage payment, in the case for example of unexpected job loss, but child support is not meant to be for that and your ex is not a bank, nor the owner of a money tree in the backyard and deep down you know that.

Chapter Five

ACCEPTING THE ARRANGED ACCESS VISIT - THE GOOD, THE BAD AND THE UGLY!

As sure as death and taxes, most custody access weekends will play out like a soap opera where everyone runs the gauntlet of emotions, from the parent dropping the kids off, to the parent having them visit, including the step-parent, grandparent, friends and the children themselves.

Most separated or divorced couples share the pick -up and drop off, and if you delight in making your ex do all the driving and making life as difficult as possible, exacting revenge in this way really has to stop.

Both parents need to work together to be able to see the children, and the children must be happy and comfortable that, while this new situation may be very different from when mum and dad were together, it is working.

More often than not, the refusal to organise a simple arrangement, where one parent drops off and the other parent picks up, stems from the fact that you just want to get back at your ex.

Maybe he or she was the one who wanted the split in the first place and your juvenile reaction is that if they want to see the kids, they have to come and get them.

But children are not silly and very quickly work out how unfair you are being.

Be honest with yourself: you are being deliberately difficult because of your split. And if it was your ex who initiated it, you see this as a way of getting back at them. Again, it will backfire on you as if the children will see their parent and/or step-parent doing all the driving they will think that they are doing their best. It is not up to your children to point this out to you.

Think of the impact of your actions on your children, and be sensible and go halves in all the to-ing and fro-ing. No matter how much bitterness there is on both sides, you need to act maturely.

Your ex has moved on — deal with it. And dealing with it, does not mean not ever setting foot on the front path of your ex's new place.

It does not mean sitting in your car at the end of their street and ringing your children when it is time to pick them up, so they are literally forced to walk down the garden path and out of the gate to trudge up to your car pulling their suitcase behind them.

Knocking on the door to pick up the children does not mean you want to be invited in for a cuppa, but parking down the street and ringing your children on their mobiles to say you're almost there is not the way to go either.

You are the parent and your ex is there —just be civil.

If their new partner opens the door, just say, "Hi, are the kids ready?" step back and let your children hear that mum or dad is being nice to the step-parent. By not doing this, you are setting the framework for the children to feel torn and to dread pick-up time.

The children also think it is very weird that mum or dad has to ring them on their phone to say they are there to pick them up, and woe betide them if they do not answer. You end up with children sitting there holding their mobiles, staring at them — and jumping and practically dropping them when they do ring.

Remember, in a child's mind things are very simple and all that stuff just adds to the strangeness and the strain of the whole situation.

If everything is still far too raw to deal with, then some simple strategies need to be implemented. Perhaps in the beginning there could be a mutually neutral place for handovers, or maybe a grandparent can act as a go-between. In an ideal world, the middle man scenario will diffuse tension, but the sooner the children can be dropped off and picked up at mum's and dad's place, the easier they will feel. It is all about putting the normal back into this new normality.

Please do not play funny games with pick-up times

either, just to get the upper hand or to prove a point that may only be in your mind. Arriving two hours early or two hours late with little notice is juvenile, schoolyard behaviour that will backfire on you.

And do not imagine that as soon as 5pm on Thursday or Friday comes, you will be free of the kids until 5pm Sunday and that you can be uncontactable.

Most children are forgetful, and children going through their parents' separation or divorce may take a few months to get into the swing of having to pack a bag on a Wednesday night because they will be going to the other parent's on Thursday after school and not return to their main home until Sunday afternoon.

Most adults would struggle to pack a bag for this routine, so you need to cut the children some slack.

Each week there will be sporting commitments, parties and occasions, and remembering absolutely everything they may need takes time to learn. In the end they will become very adaptable travellers and very efficient packers, but in the beginning it is difficult.

What perhaps makes it even more difficult is if a child forgets a sports uniform needed on a weekend and has been told that once they leave their main home, they are not allowed back until the drop-off on Sunday night. Their key is taken away, probably because the parent does not want their ex to set foot in what is now their house, and that is fair enough. However, the real reason may be that the parent has met someone else and does not want the children to know they are seeing them yet. And that is fine. It really is.

But surely the child can give the parent a call if they have forgotten anything and something can be worked out? So the parent can drop off the stuff or, if enough notice is given, the child can go back inside what is their familiar territory? Maybe an old uniform could be kept at the step-parent's place just in case it is ever needed?

And here is a thought: it may well be your weekend off, but if you have two children and one child's football match is across town and the other child's sporting commitment is literally a few streets away from you with both scheduled at the same time, if you are not really doing anything on that weekend, would it kill you to offer to help out on this rare occasion? After all it is your child. This does not mean it has to become a habit, nor that the other parent should expect it or take liberties in the future if the going gets tough. But I will never forget a rowing commitment in Geelong, while there was another less than five minutes away from my stepchildren's mother's house. Luckily another parent came to the rescue as I had to work, but it would have been far simpler if a little flexibility had been shown! Nights can always be swapped at a later date, but for my stepson to only be five minutes from the football ground at 8am would have made far more sense. And no, his mother had no special weekend planned. The extra night could easily have been tacked onto the following visit.

Perhaps the most helpful piece of advice I can give anyone is:

Leave your mobile phone on!

I believe it is fair to assume nowadays that most people, especially parents, have a mobile phone. In fact, it is very difficult to function without a mobile. Many schools send out bulk texts, and if you do not have a mobile you are basically stuffed and cannot operate.

If your children are going to the other parent for the weekend, it is not an opportunity to switch off your mobile because you may think that technically you are not on duty.

You know full well that you are on duty as a parent 24/7 for the rest of your life and have been since they were born!

There are numerous things that can crop up during a custody weekend, from a trip to a doctor to clarification on something. For example, where or when the specific match or birthday party is.

You also need another copy of your Medicare and/or private health insurance cards for your ex so that they can keep one just in case.

It never ceased to amaze me that when my husband's ex wanted something she would ring at all hours, yet during those custody weekends the message bank was in full swing or the phone was simply switched off and calls never returned.

It's all ancient history now, but it could have been sorted out easily.

As the step-parent you are continually juggling and sometimes second-guessing yourself.

While you may feel uneasy about the ex knocking on your door to drop off or pick up the children, grin and bear it. Be polite and keep it brief.

Let the children see and hear that you are being nice to their mum or dad. Otherwise you set the framework for the kids to feel torn and dread the drop off or pick-up time.

Just do not feel guilty. It is normal to feel apprehensive about your stepchildren visiting. Suddenly, your home is being turned upside down to accommodate children who visit every alternate week or have a routine such as alternate Thursday to Sunday nights.

Do not feel guilty. It is normal to feel like a stranger in your own home at times and even to resent these children coming over what may sometimes feel like all the time! It does not mean you hate your step kids. Far from it, it means you are feeling like everyone else in the step-parenting conundrum.

If you do not have your own children you sometimes feel even more at sea, ganged up on because in the beginning it is suddenly just your partner and their kids and you. You may be bending over backwards making an effort, yet often feel you are getting nowhere — washing, cooking, tidying, taxiing, biting your tongue when you feel awkward, wanting but not wanting to discipline bad behaviour which is obvious to you but seems to have gone unnoticed for perhaps years!

But you can only control what happens in your home. You have no control over what has gone on or been said at their other home during the previous week . It is difficult, but try not to take niggly behaviour personally, especially when the children first arrive.

They will have no doubt been subjected to an instructional drilling on the drive over to your place and be confused, especially if you have always been nice to them.

On one hand they have got mum or dad telling them that you are not their mum or dad so not to do what you tell them to, yet on the other they know you have been kind and nice to them and they are trying their best to adjust, and so they feel torn when they should not.

There will be times when you have slaved away making cakes, muffins, sandwiches and dinners and you won't get a thank you. As annoying as it is, don't retaliate. Remember, the parent they are living with most of the time may have pumped them up during the drive over, reminding them to be as difficult as possible. All you can do is lead by example and try not to take things personally. This may take many months or even years to really understand.

There will also be times when you have to drive your stepchildren to a party or job or sporting commitment. Deep down, they will think it cool their stepmum or stepdad is taking them to a party or even to their school football match, but you must be prepared for them not to show emotion. Although the fact you are putting yourself out for them does not go unnoticed, it may not be acknowledged.

If you are the other parent, you have to face up to the fact that, regardless of how it happened, your ex has moved on.

You can either churn over it for the rest of your life or go for counselling and recognise that no matter how the break up occurred, some of the blame falls on you, even if you do not want to admit it. Take your head out of the sand and start being objective.

Very few people can accept their failures, work on them and move on to a happier life. People dwell, bitch, plan revenge and spend more time being negative than drawing that line in the sand and trying to progress.

A successful future relationship is in your own interests. You need to be happy. No one else can wave a magic wand and take away the hurt of a break up. You need to work on yourself. Your next partner does not want to become embroiled in all this stuff. They will want to see the type of person you are and get to know you.

Ultimately, you must think of the impact your behaviour is having on your children and/or stepchildren.

You may wonder if there actually is such thing as a happy step-family or whether it is just an illusion. I think there is or I would not have written this book.

Someone suggested the following:

"Perhaps if both people have moved on with other people there may be an opportunity for a once-a-year park BBQ so all the children can have a chance to see some normality in adult relationships.

"Naturally each person would have to have really sorted themselves out and sorted out any emotional feelings and be completely over the last relationship, but the park BBQ is an idea at least."

Initially I tried to put myself in that dynamic, and while my husband's ex-wife is the last person I ever want to see, I would have done it for the sake of my stepchildren. They are now adults so it is too late, but when they were 11 and 12 I would have done it. Unfortunately our situation was not conducive to anything like that. Future weddings will no doubt be the next battleground!

Step-parenting is all about what children see, how it is filtered and how we react.

You will get frustrated, upset, angry — because at the end of the day there is no such thing as a perfect step-family, just as there is no such thing as a perfect family.

It is all about having a workable situation with balance and respect for everyone in a new reality, coupled with a strong desire to achieve the very best outcome. Sometimes you will and sometimes you won't — it is a continual learning curve for everyone involved.

One of the most amazing occasions I have ever attended was the first birthday of the daughter of a girlfriend of mine, amazing because:

My friend was 30 years old. Her mum had married and had her at 17, and then had her brother at 19. She divorced soon after my friend was born, but went on to marry another man whom my friend always called Dad as he had been in her life since she was 18 months old.

Her mother and step-father divorced when my friend was 17. Although she had met her biological father twice, she regarded her stepfather as her father as he had fed and clothed her, etc.

Her mother, aged 47, went on to marry a man in his 60s.

Her stepfather married a woman 20 years younger, the same age as my friend.

Her mother remained in South Africa and her step-father emigrated to Australia. My friend got married in England and then she and her husband emigrated to Australia.

At the time of my friend's daughter's first birthday, her stepfather was 50, his new wife was 30, the same age as my friend, and she was expecting twins.

So in my friend's house there were her mother, her mother's new husband, her stepdad and his new wife, heavily pregnant with twins.

The dynamic was that she and her stepmum are exactly the same age! She considers the twins, who were born a couple of months later, as her brother and sister, but 30 years younger.

And they were able to put all differences aside and get together for my friend's daughter's first birthday.

Her mother and stepfather did not sit next to each

other, but they certainly realised that the occasion was the important thing, not them.

When her stepfather's twins were born, her mum rang her ex-husband and his new wife and sent genuine congratulations.

I sat there in awe of this real-life dynamic which could have been an episode from an American TV sitcom. So if we behave well there is hope for us all!

– Chapter Six –

A NEW BABY

Sooner or later, you have to face the fact that your ex-partner is indeed having sex again. And, whether they have remarried or are in a de facto relationship, if their new partner becomes pregnant, yes, your ex is now having sex!

It seems to be the one thing that people involved in break-ups cannot accept.

When a baby comes along, it changes everything.

More often than not, people do not want to have anything to do with their ex and even advocate the separation and/or divorce. But as soon as their ex becomes involved with someone else, it is as if they have forgotten that sex and passion are part of a new relationship, and sometimes a baby is born sooner than either party planned.

The parent:

When a baby is born, it can be tricky. If you are the female ex-partner of a man, and his new partner has given birth and you yourself are already a mum, do not take your anger out on the first-time mum and make life difficult for her. You are angry because your ex having sex is a reality when a new baby is born.

Even if his new partner has children of her own from an earlier relationship, show some compassion.

Compassion may be the last thing you want to show, but if you have an alternate fortnight custody arrangement, you could make a gesture and keep the kids for an extra month. The time can be made up later on.

Do not kid yourself it's important for the children to feel involved. Indeed it is, but someone who has given birth is exhausted, and the last thing they want is anyone hanging around, no matter how well meaning.

If you've given birth, I am sure on the day you came home from the hospital, you didn't want anyone around except your partner. I used to believe that all the children are brothers and sisters, however now I think it adds to unnecessary confusion.

It is not a matter of always poignantly or dogmatically referring to the half-brother or half-sister — perhaps not saying it is easier in the long run. We call them the big kids and the little kids.

If you are a father and ex-wife has a baby with her new partner, you may also experience some resentful feelings, but you should be just as accommodating as if positions were reversed.

Denying your children the chance to go to the hospital to meet their new baby brother or sister is cruel.

Even if the birth happens to be midweek or on an alternate weekend, be the bigger person and let your ex take them for a visit.

I have seen the damage done when they have been denied meeting the baby simply because their own mum's jealousy overrides the fact that all these children are now related forever.

If you have young children, filling their head with poison and your own frustration will be counterproductive in the long run — and good can come out of every situation, whatever you may feel.

If you have disparaged your ex's new son or daughter, you are forgetting that long after you are both dead your own children will still be related to them.

Most children get excited about a new baby, although the ex is not going to be pleased at all. Children do not have the same baggage and anger. They are waiting anxiously, curiously, a little bit excitedly and maybe nervously for their new sibling.

As the stepparent, it is tricky to know how you will feel after giving birth, but depending on their maturity and age and how you are feeling, do allow your stepchildren to visit you in the hospital.

A step family is all about inclusion, and making children feel part of something is always a good thing.

Before you have the baby, you could ask them what names they like and why. If they are nothing like the names you have chosen, maybe mention one and ask if they like it. Perhaps you could use one of the names they have chosen as a middle name.

You will need to sit them down at some stage and explain that there will be some adjusting necessary with a newborn in the house and they may need to be a little quieter at times. But reassure them they will be a big brother or sister and involve them as much as you can, depending on their reaction.

Explain to them that as you are now a parent, it's a new ball game and you may be on edge, worried or protective, remembering to add the crucial phrase "just as your mum and dad must have been when you were born."

Do not feel guilty if in the initial couple of months you do not feel the same when your stepchildren are around. It has nothing to do with resentment. In this bonding period, all you really want is to be with your partner and the new baby.

Emotions after childbirth can be overwhelming. Dealing with stepchildren and extended family is difficult, but it is all part and parcel of life. If you feel this way you are not a bad person, but your emotions and hormones are working overtime and having to think of anyone except your new baby is the last thing you want.

It is difficult enough juggling your own children with the arrival of a newborn.

My stepson was 14 and my stepdaughter was 13 when our son was born, so there was none of the jealousy you might get with little children. Be mindful though that if you have toddlers and a new baby, you may need to give extra reassurance that they are all part of it.

For a step-parent it is a huge realisation that you will never really get the time alone that you crave. Your needs come second, and unhelpful comments from ill-informed people like "you knew what you were getting into when you became a stepmother/step-parent," do not help.

As a step-parent, everyone else's needs are put above yours and you have to keep the peace 99 per cent of the time.

The new baby is related to your children and always will be. If you start off not allowing them to see the new baby if they want to, that bodes ill for the future.

When our daughter was born, my stepdaughter was not allowed to come to the hospital after school, but my stepson happened to have a day off and my husband brought him to see us.

This was never mentioned, but I know my stepdaughter was upset at being the only one who had not seen the baby. She and her brother were about to go on holiday with their mother and it was only a month later that she met her half-sister.

Letting your children pop into the hospital to meet the new arrival really should not be that big a deal.

Financially, when a new baby arrives there are always

adjustments. There may be arguments, there may not —
but there are always adjustments.

If you are the parent here is something to ponder: if
your children have been lucky enough to be accepted by
your ex-partner's new partner and made to feel part of a
new family, you should be very thankful as it could easily
have gone the other way.

Some step-parents choose to ignore your children
whom they see as a threat to their new relationship with
your ex. That is not right or good at all and needs to be
rectified as soon as possible. However, in my experience
all the new stepparent wants is to make things work for
everyone.

If your children have been lucky enough to have their
own bedroom and now have to share a bedroom, or if
one now has to sleep on a sofa bed, writing threatening
legal letters will do no good.

In most divorces, the mother keeps the family home,
even if that means a massive mortgage. You are both re-
building your lives, but ironically if one of you meets a
new partner who has also gone through a separation or
divorce and lost his family home to his ex-wife or partner,
you will get a better perspective.

Ask yourself if three nights a fortnight mean your
children must have a bedroom each? What about the new
baby, who needs a routine and some uninterrupted time?

A little perspective: if your child has to sleep on a
pull out bed for the three nights they spend at your ex's

because the bedroom has to be converted into a nursery for a newborn, it's not ideal but what can they do?

Just be happy your children have another loving home to go to, because leaving a bedroom empty for 11 out of 14 nights is not right once a new baby comes along. We all have to pitch in and make do. That is what life is all about.

– Chapter Seven –

TAMING THAT GREEN-EYED MONSTER

There is something to be said for jealousy. Everyone denies they are jealous, but it's amazing how actions speak louder than words.

The fact that you do not want to be with your partner any more is one thing, but as soon as they move on with someone else, the green-eyed monster raises its head.

As a parent it is now more crucial than ever that you control irrational behaviour before it backfires.

If you had two children with your ex-partner, until they have more children the scales of power are tipped in your favour, although most step-parents do not want any form of power play. They just want to get on with life as peacefully as possible and make the whole situation work.

If you had a son and a daughter with your ex-partner and they remarried and had another son and daughter in the same order, how would you react?

Everyone has a 50-50 chance of having a boy or a girl, and thinking the ex and his new partner are copying what you did many years ago is what I call bonkers behaviour and defies rational thought.

I hope you would not react this way because you think you have been spited and that there is a conspiracy against you.

This chapter has been the most challenging and uncomfortable to write in case it is seen as inflammatory. I toyed with the idea of leaving it out, but this is not a book that shies away from challenging step-parenting situations.

There is often a 'he said-she said' (or a 'she said-she said') scenario. Some people will try to find an excuse for everything that happens.

What goes around comes around. I hope to stop irrational behaviour from people wanting to get back at their ex-partner, the new partner and their children — who will always be related to their half-brothers and sisters.

My 13-year old stepdaughter had tested positive for whooping cough. She came over to our house for the normal custody arrangement of one week during the holidays, and my husband was not told, even though his ex-wife had told her family, including her sister who had a baby the same age ours, to stay away due to infection.

The ex-wife's father and brother were both pharmacists and she worked in a pharmacy they owned, so was well aware of the seriousness of whooping cough for a baby.

As a result my step-daughter came to stay when we were caring for our 12-week-old baby girl who could not be immunised against whooping cough until she was 12 months old, and was therefore deliberately placed at severe risk of infection.

When it turned out that my step-daughter did indeed have whooping cough, her mother refused to have her back home because this was her father's week.

When something like this happens you cannot be rigid in your approach to custody arrangements.

My stepdaughter should have been back home with her mother in isolation. Her mother had no specific plans that week and we could have had my stepdaughter for an extra week down the track.

Health is paramount for all families, especially for young children who are at higher risk, and my 15-month-old son, despite being fully immunised, did contract whooping cough from my stepdaughter. Treatment was delayed because of her mother's decision not to tell her father that she had it. Even though our 15-month-old had a cough and red cheeks, when the doctor asked if anyone in the family had whooping cough, I said no. My step-daughter often had a sniffle and was going through the teenage stage of wearing light clothing and thongs after netball. Whooping cough never even entered our minds.

If her father had been told, a simple course of preventative antibiotics for everyone might have saved numerous trips to the doctor — because my husband and I caught it too.

The doctor told me that is actually not uncommon — just a new weapon in the war of separation and divorce.

Other friends told us later that the same thing had happened to them when their son was six.

Anger was only one emotion. I could hardly believe that a woman with two children of her own would do that. Warning people to stay away from a contagious disease is a normal thing to do.

I had always looked after her children with care and kindness as if they were my own, and she would not even have her daughter back while she was in quarantine because it was 'the father's week for custody.'

In my generation, mumps, measles and whooping cough were well known to be serious. My stepdaughter said she didn't realise how serious it was, and that made me even angrier. There are plenty of examples of the damage that these illnesses do and we are now constantly informed about the dangers.

My husband says my stepdaughter still feels bad about the whole thing, especially as she loves her younger brother, but she has never said anything to me.

This was the only time I ever yelled at my stepdaughter and berated her. When she has children of her own, I am sure she will look back at the incident and realise why I acted the way I did.

It was our only argument and she later had a long talk to her father and cleared up a range of issues, so we resumed on an even keel.

Throughout the whole whooping cough episode I was very angry and I am writing from my own point of view as a voice for others.

If you are an ex reading this who has not moved on yet, taking anger out in this or indeed any way does not help anyone...

Is there a moral to this chapter? Well, I finally realised that there would never be peace between myself and my husband's ex-wife until this was resolved with an apology and acknowledgement. My husband was just as upset that someone he had previously married and had two children with was capable of acting like this.

After this episode a line was drawn in the sand. How could there not be.

There is a difference in having respect for someone because their children are our future and having respect for someone.

I respect my husband's ex-wife as a mother, but not otherwise. This is ironic though, because her partner has a young son and daughter, and their mother has inflicted the same pain on her as she has on me. You never know when your life will change and mirror a given situation — or when a mother will become a stepmother herself.

STEP-PARENTING WITH PURPOSE

Can the warring parties ever reach neutral ground?

Even when the ex moves on and meets someone else, and you think there may be a thawing now that both people have re-partnered, that a wedding or a christening might be ok, do not kid yourself.

Several friends have asked me whether I would go to my stepchildren's weddings if I were invited. I just don't know. It is their day, and if having me there would make it difficult for them and overshadow the whole thing, I would respect that and be mature enough to realise the difficulties that may be there and make an informed, respectful decision. The last thing I would want is for them to feel torn with the added stress that so often materialises during these life events. Ever spoken to the adult children of divorced or separated parents and the stress they themselves feel in trying to organise table seating, photographs and so on to try and keep the peace? It is an eye opener.

Many people say I must go and that they would be adults. The reality when it comes to weddings and blended family dynamics is very different in each situation. You just have to take each day as it comes and see how it all goes. Things can turn on a dime, but despite the input a step-parent may have made, more often than not the stepchild's primary loyalties still lie with their mother and a father.

My husband would always go, that's a given. But for me, until that apology comes over the whole whooping cough incident, which really was one of the triggers for our interstate move, it is still raw.

All this may seem contradictory because here I am writing a book on step-parenting to help others face the situations I have been through, but I am not an expert although I am always open to seeing if there is a middle ground and a possible resolution.

The step-family is a real and everchanging thing, but for many a step-parent, you sort of fade into the background on occasion, however long you have had stepchildren for. And a wedding day should not be overshadowed by tension.

But all this is hypothetical. There are no engagements or weddings on the horizon. I have always wished my stepchildren the very best and I hope I helped enrich their upbringing, taught them things and loved them. I will always be there for them when they want help or advice, but I am a step-parent and stepchildren are not your own.

Weddings are a minefield at the best of times and sometimes it is better just to stay right out.

A step-parent does not have the same rights as a parent or guardian. You may have put your heart and soul into it, but you are still not their mother or father, although if you marry someone who has been widowed that is slightly different.

The sooner people realise this the easier life becomes for everyone.

It really all comes down to respect.

Respect both for and from your stepchildren, respect for their mother or father, and self-respect.

I have always told my stepchildren that they should treat people the way they have been treated, regardless of whether their mother or father likes that person. If their stepmother or stepfather is nice to them, be nice back! They know that it is highly unlikely their mother or father really likes their step-parent, but that may change one day.

Be thankful if the new partner of your ex-partner is kind to your children, accepts the custody arrangement and does not try to stop them seeing each other. It could easily have gone the other way and your ex-partner turned against you and your children.

Get over your jealousy and remember that while you have no connection to your ex-partner's new children, your own children do. Do you want them to end up on *Find My Family* television shows because you have prevented a relationship developing between the children?

Perhaps the greater the age gap the more important it is to bear all this in mind.

They say prejudice does not exist in little children, it is learned. Everyone in the family needs to adjust to the situation when new children are added to the mix. It should not be a competition.

The following two quotes are worth remembering:

"Being a step-parent is learning about strengths you did not know you had and dealing with fears you never knew existed."

"Being a step-parent means the children will always have another person who will teach them and love them for who they actually are."

There is room for everyone in this new stepfamily dynamic and there always will be. If you keep communication open and forget playing games, everything works a lot better.

— Chapter Eight —

TURNING HOLIDAY HELL INTO HOLIDAY HEAVEN!

It never ceases to amaze me what a battleground the holidays become, and that changes depending on the age of the children you are step-parenting. However, holidays need not be a warzone.

Over the years, we did most holiday combinations: two weeks on, two weeks off, two weeks on, two weeks off over summer — four weeks on, four weeks off and even one week on, one week off for the eight consecutive summer holiday weeks.

The 48-hour Christmas and Boxing Day period meant a taxi service for both sides and was quite miserable, but no one ever used that word.

If you live interstate or overseas, most years one parent has the kids for Christmas and the New Year and the other the following year.

But when we all lived in the same state the battle lines were drawn every Christmas.

Just to complicate things, my husband's birthday is on Christmas Eve and his court orders said he wanted his children to spend his birthday with him.

One year the children were dropped off at his ex's at 8pm on Christmas Eve, picked up at 10am on Christmas morning, taken back at 3pm that afternoon and then picked up again at 8am on Boxing Day.

It was insane, especially given the military precision timing of when to leave and how to navigate the traffic.

The reason was nothing to do with opening presents from Santa. It boiled down to the fact that if the children stayed overnight on Christmas Eve, that might have meant one day less child support based on the annual nights. Ridiculous!

I think all parents need to be both practical and reasonable in considering alternate Christmases, so the kids are in the same place for Christmas Eve, Christmas Day and Boxing Day.

You could volunteer at a Christmas charity homeless lunch. And take your children along too before you hand them over. That soon brings everyone down to earth.

The power games that are played at this time of year are incredible. There needs to be some flexibility.

It is fair enough to swap holidays come New Year's Eve, but this generation will think spending most of Christmas Day shuffling in and out of cars and going from this house to that house watching the clock is normal.

Everyone needs to take a good hard look, and the kids should have happy memories of Christmas — not constant stress and tension.

On our first post-divorce Christmas Day as my husband pulled up in his ex-in-laws' driveway his ex-wife was screaming down the phone. The children still remember it. Relax and use your common sense. Treat everyone with the courtesy and respect you expect.

Would you want your ex exceeding the speed limit and risk running into the back of a truck for a few unimportant minutes?

The children already think splitting Christmas and the holidays is weird, and this is about taking the weirdness out of it as much as possible.

Children know that if Dad is dropping them off at Mum's and she has already made that where are they phone call, she will be in a bad mood and they will be the ones who cop it from her — and no doubt her side of the family — once they go inside. Remember, this is the next generation we want to hold up an example to.

Christmas is merely one stressful holiday. Other celebrations in other cultures and religions can also turn into virtual emotional war games. Try and find common ground and understanding.

The courts are there for a reason, but why make the lawyers even richer when you can all sit down and find a solution for the holidays. But if arguments, tension and stress are rising, then you need a third party to help.

Children want a happy Christmas. All the presents in the world will not make up for their parents fighting over specific days and hours.

The actual day will come and go, but the memory of what it was like will last for years. They will not remember the latest Barbie, Beanie Boo, Lego, electronic game or clothes they receive, but they will always remember the screaming and yelling.

Parenting is not a competition. We should all be on the same side, the side that loves and supports the child. Look at yourself own actions and show this generation the right way to behave.

– Chapter Nine –

WHEN IT COMES TO PRESENTS, WHAT DO I DO?

Presents are always tricky. The new partner wants their step children to like them, so there is a tendency to spend more than necessary.

We have all fallen into this trap, even as parents, but it is important to nip it in the bud, otherwise you will be trapped for years and always wonder if they like you or the gifts.

It all depends on the children's ages but, from my experience, just remembering their birthdays and Christmas and other religious celebrations with an appropriate card and gift is enough.

You do not need to spend a fortune — being thoughtful is the point, and acknowledging that they are into sports or animals or their favourite music.

One of my first gifts to my stepdaughter cost $5. It was a large magnetic pinboard with doggy footprints over it and markers, a lovely photo frame with I love my dog on it and a $2 Puppies and Dogs calendar.

They were an instant hit and the tradition of buying the $2 Puppies and Dogs calendar was born.

My stepdaughter was already getting loads of presents from the extended family. I did not want to overstep the mark to win her admiration or draw a rebuke from anyone. So many children get so many gifts that they often get lost on the day, and it is not the monetary value of a gift that is important, it is the thought.

I wanted to recognise her as an individual and acknowledge her favourite things and favourite colours.

I had not known her that long, but my gifts showed that I had noticed that she was madly into puppies and dogs and adored her own dog, and it wasn't the look-at-me gift that many step-parents first give.

I got my stepson an Adidas-3 striped baseball cap and matching T-shirt. He is sports mad and it was a gift he would use.

Your partner's children usually have aunts and uncles, cousins, grandparents and in some cases great-grandparents as well as their own mother and father, so they are hardly going to go without.

After my stepchildren reached 18, the separate presents from me — with the exception of a 21st keepsake —stopped and all presents were a proper joint gift from their father and me.

Their dad was always very generous, and in those early years I did not want to make them feel that their gift was from us both. It was their dad's chance to get them what they wanted.

Not everyone will do it the way I did, but do not go overboard as a step-parent. Children see through anything that is not genuine. Let them like you for remembering their birthday rather than the gift.

They were 11 and 12 years old when I first met them and I believe I did a good job of always finding appropriate birthday cards.

My stepson was sports mad and I always found good sports cards, and for my stepdaughter I always found cute dog cards.

I did not spend a lot of money as their father bought the main present, but I found thoughtful gifts that were always used and never just left in their wrapping. I also never wanted to upstage their mother or buy them anything that she would not buy.

At Christmas I got the small knick-knacky stocking fillers and my husband bought their main presents, and we told them that they were from both of us but that I was better at stocking fillers and they agreed! One year, I made photo albums for them.

When we had our own children, initially I did a $2 shop birthday card from them to their big brother and sister, and as the children grew older they made their own cards and gifts for them.

If you are a parent and your son or daughter is jumping up and down with excitement about a new toy or something given to them by your ex-partner's new partner, even if you know you could not afford it or had never even thought of it, do not let that green-eyed monster raise its head.

Just say "that's nice, darling," and that is all you need to say (YouTube the Mrs Brown's Boys' *That's nice* episode again!).

Save your bitching for a cuppa with your girlfriends away from the children's ears, and remember, you are assigning motives through adult understanding; the child simply sees a great present they have received.

But people are always looking for ulterior motives and a gift to your children from the new partner is really done nine times out of 10 for the child, not to get back at you.

And be careful with your reactions. If you get into the game of showing your displeasure at what your ex-partner's new partner has given your child at birthdays and Christmas, that will set up deceptive behaviour for the future.

Children are very quick at learning the lie of the land and what to tell one parent and not the other.

When my husband and I went to London as part of our honeymoon, we found a Liverpool football flag and shoe bag for footy boots as a great 13th birthday present for my stepson. I felt like I was onto a winner — teenage boys are difficult to buy for at the best of times.

I was stunned by his reaction —bad temper and tears — completely out of character and it was very unlike him not to be grateful.

I got very upset myself and burst into tears, wondering

who the adult was. Had I got the wrong thing? Was it last year's logo? What went wrong?

However, the whole issue and reason for the meltdown was "But what do I say to my mum when she asks who gave it to me?"

"Just say your dad gave it to you, "I replied.

And then, came the crunch line: "But that's wrong, isn't it, KT? It's lying," he said.

"Yes, you're right," I replied. "But if you know your mum won't be happy that I have given you something, it's the easiest way for you to keep the peace."

And that was how it was resolved, and indeed how every other birthday and Christmas present was explained.

To me, that was very sad indeed, and proof that children in this situation are acutely aware of the intricacies of what goes on.

His reaction to the gift was not normal, but given the fact he had heard and been involved in knowing what was going on between his mother and father, it was normal for him. He had evidently overheard his mother talking about the step-parent in a derogatory way, to someone else and as much as he wanted to be able to say his step-mother had thought of him on a trip, he was searching for ways to hide it as he knew what the reaction would be.

Child Support:

Everyone has their own view on Australia's Child Support Agency (CSA).

Regardless of that view, Child Support is a legal obligation to be paid until a child turns 18. There are certain circumstances in some states where it continues until the end of the school year once the child turns 18 or if the child has special needs.

The following information is from the Australian Child Support Agency website and other Australian government sources, correct at the time of going to print. May I please reiterate this waiver, that the purpose of using this general information is for guidance only and you must seek official advice pertinent to your own personal circumstances. No responsibility is held by myself or the publisher for anyone's Child Support obligations as required under Australian law. You must seek official advice.

You are paying child support because it is a parent's responsibility to financially support a child.

Child support is normally worked out based on the taxable incomes of parents, the percentage of nights each parent has the child or children per year, the number of children aged less than 13 years old and the number aged 13-17 years old and any information based on any other dependents.

The incomes of parents are an essential part of calculating child support in Australia.

The formula uses taxable income which is the income the parent reports to the Australian Taxation Office (ATO) when submitting their annual tax return.

It is your gross, before-tax income rather than net income. The child support formula uses the taxable income reported in the parent's most recent tax return.

However, the formula assumes each parent needs a certain amount of income to maintain themselves. This is calculated as one third of annualised Male Total Average Weekly Earnings (MTAWE). For example, in 2019, the Self Support Amount was $25,038.

So, if a father has a $75,000 taxable income, his fixed Self Support Amount is $25,000 (one third of MTAWE), meaning $50,000 is the child support income for the average man in Australia.

For a mother who has a $50,000 taxable income, the fixed Self Support Amount is $25,000, meaning $25,000 is the child support income for the average woman in Australia.

The table used combines the child support incomes of both parents, the number and ages of the children and, using the above examples ($50,000 + $25,000) and one child, this means that child support works out at around $19,500 a year.

The support goes up with income, and children aged more than 13 receive about 20 per cent more. Second and third children get about half the amount of the first child.

There is no extra paid for more than three children.

Then there are the income shares and income percentage for each parent.

The income percentage is calculated from parent incomes, and is the percentage of costs a parent is responsible for.

For example, if the mother's child support income is $25,000 and the combined child support income is $75,000, the income percentage is 33.3 per cent.

If the father's child income support is $50,000 and the combined child support income is $75,000, it equals 66.7 per cent.

A parent is also credited with a percentage of costs for looking after the child or children, depending on the number of nights they spend with a parent. This is calculated using a Care and Cost Table.

Example 1. Mum has the child nine out of 14 nights, which equals 64 per cent .

The child is in her care for 64 per cent of the time, so she gets 73 per cent of the cost.

Example 2. Dad has the child five nights out of 14, which equals 36 per cent .

The child is in his care for 36 per cent of the time, so he gets 27 per cent of the cost.

This shows us how much child support is paid and how much is received.

Using the same example, if the cost to the father of the children is $19,500 x (66.7 per cent income less 27 per cent cost) that is $7,735. If the cost to the mother, usually the primary carer, is $19,500 x (73 per cent cost of care less 33.3 per cent income) she receives $7,735.

The above is merely a generic example and I take no responsibility in terms of child support obligations a parent may legally face, but it shows that if you are in the midst of a divorce and child support becomes a reality, it really is a whole new playing field.

There may also be a separate agreement for school fees, school camps, school uniforms, school stationery, etc.

Suddenly having to account for all your income and expenses and have them documented by a third party – in this case a government agency – causes many parents shock, panic and a sense of entitlement. Some parents think they are paying too much while the other person thinks that they are not paying enough and often a vicious cycle of discussion, disagreement and argument ensues.

For every parent paying the child support they owe, many others are part of a large, systemic problem of not paying.

Services Australia, formerly known as the Department of Human Services, is in charge of recovering child support debt and has wide powers to recover the money, working with third parties such as an employer, issuing an overseas travel ban and intercepting tax refunds.

However, the day-to-day reality for anyone who has been owed child support is that there are parents who quit their jobs and become self-employed to lower the sum, or move assets and income elsewhere to reduce the amount of their taxable income.

Recent media reports show around $1.5 billion outstanding in child support in Australia. About 85 per cent of child support recipients are women, so most of this huge debt is owed by dads.

More than half of all child support is paid privately, meaning the figure is much higher.

A recent parliamentary inquiry showed that 36 per cent of child support transferred by the CSA in 2014 was $500 or less per year, or about $1 per day.

Of the 272,000 parents asked to pay this tiny amount, 60,000 were in arrears.

None of this augurs well for anyone, let alone the children who need a safe, secure and supportive environment.

Leaving rogue elements to one side, I want to focus on the conduct of the recipient of child support — mostly, but not exclusively, women.

As I mentioned earlier, child support is for your children. It is not to pay off your mortgage, rent, utilities and so on. You would be paying them regardless and this is one of the main things that annoys parents paying child support. They are not a bank for your lifestyle; they are looking after their offspring to the best of their ability and, in sharing support for your children, hope that you will continue to look after them.

If you are one of the fortunate parents whose ex does

pay child support, you are lucky to have a responsible ex. So as a step-parent, I beg you not to send your children on their custody visit without sufficient clothes, shoes, clean underwear or personal hygiene amenities so that your ex has to pay for them.

This is an unnecessary form of emotional blackmail.

My husband and I never had this problem, perhaps because the children were slightly older and had a good handle on what they needed for their weekend visits, but many people spend money on clothes they never see again when their ex is playing games.

I always told my stepchildren to help their mum around the house as she was working as well and always refrained from digs – as my youngest daughter would say "Zip it, lock it and put it in your pocket!"

Grandparents:

These are challenging times for grandparents as their own safe worlds are torn apart, and many do lose contact with their grandchildren.

Grandparents often ask what they should do about presents. It sounds like a minefield at first, but only takes a few moments to think it through.

Your son or daughter has two children, separates or divorces and then they meet someone with another child or children.

Of course as a grandparent you do not have to spend the same amount on the new partner's children as you would on your own grandchildren, but do accept them in the same way that you would want your own grandchildren to be accepted by that new partner's parents.

Don't nit-pick. If your son or daughter's new partner has one child and perhaps their own parents are dead and/or their ex-partner's too, you may want to spend more as if their child were your own. That is fine and you can do as you please, but usually there are other grandparents in the picture.

People get all tied up in knots.

I believe that if you are spending $50 per grandchild, you do not need to fork out $50 on the new partner's child.

But you do need to get them something. Every child wants a present at Christmas.

A little advice for the new girlfriend, boyfriend, husband or wife: many grandparents are on a pension and cannot afford much. You will know when you see how your new or potential in-laws live.

If you are the new partner who has children from a previous relationship, it is up to you to tell them your kids get plenty and it's not necessary.

You may say that your child does not have children of their own, but they have met someone who does, and what do you do now that you are a sort of grandparent?

Essentially, it is up to you. Maybe your son or daughter wants to legally adopt the child or children. Or it may just be accepted that they will be referred to as theirs, and hence your grandchildren. Nothing has to be written in stone.

I knew someone who had three biological grandchildren, and their son met a woman with three children of her own.

Suddenly the $50 per grandchild out of their pension at Christmas was going to become $300 if they spent the same on the partner's children as on her own.

Luckily the mother of the children was pretty savvy, had thought a few steps ahead and was so relieved her new partner's mother had accepted her and her children that she took the advice I have given and told the woman that really was not necessary for her to buy Christmas presents as her children had other extended family.

I had also told her that the reason why the woman had lost so much weight recently was because she had been missing meals to be able to save money for Christmas to buy the children gifts. True story.

Their mother was absolutely horrified, and so was her partner, the woman's son, who had never imagined this.

The suggestion of a $10 trinket from this grandparent ended up meaning more to them than anything.

A little while later they married, and it became a real Brady Bunch as they both then had a child together, giving the grandmother another biological grandchild.

As time goes by, it all sorts itself out, but in the initial stages try and remember how difficult it is for older people to find the money for extra gifts.

There is no one size fits all approach to this situation.

What I have outlined is merely an observation over the years of situations that have arisen from friends and acquaintances' experiences in step-parenting.

You do what you feel is right. But you also reap what you sow. If you completely ignore your child's new partner's children, it may well be counterproductive and turn them against you. Generosity comes in many ways. it does not always have to be material or a monetary gift. Spending an hour cooking muffins in your kitchen or a trip to the nearest park may have a far more lasting impact.

The stepchild:

Perhaps a little advice for the stepchild to consider?

Okay, so your mum and dad are unlikely to take you to the shops to buy a present for your stepparent, meaning their new partner. If they do, then you should feel very lucky that your parents are showing you the correct way to behave.

Whether it is your stepmother or stepfather's birthday or an important occasion, I really do think you should acknowledge it by more than simply saying something. Buying a card from the $2 shop is enough, or a trinket, depending on your age. You are old enough to realise that if your step-parent has been good to you, you should do something nice for them.

You are savvy enough to know whether your mum and dad get on once they have split.

If there is little communication, but you visit the other parent and their new partner regularly, you do not have to say what you bought your step-parent if that will rub salt in the wound.

This is not being deceptive at all —and you all know what I am talking about.

Some mums and dads will pretend that, despite your spending every alternate weekend with your parent and their new partner, the new partner simply does not exist. But you know that is not the case.

Most of the time the stepparent is trying their very best to create a happy, harmonious workable step-parenting family situation every time you come over.

Acknowledgement rather than monetary might is the true key.

A picture drawn for your step-parent says more than a thousand words.

A cake you make says more than one bought from a shop.

A hug and a smile will make any step-parent's day.

Chapter Ten

MOTHER'S DAY, FATHER'S DAY AND ANY OTHER OCCASION YOU CAN THINK OF!

You have probably gathered that what one person thinks is just common sense, another thinks of as the complete opposite!

Despite an alternate custody arrangement at weekends, I always imagined that if Father's Day happened to fall on the other parent's weekend, common sense would dictate they simply swap.

Surprisingly, this is often not the case — sometimes out of sheer spite, and in the end whom does it benefit? Certainly not the children.

Sadly this nasty pattern behaviour becomes ingrained and does not do the children any good in their future relationships as adults.

I have to come to realise that it is unrealistic to expect the other parent to take a child out to buy a gift or card for their mother or father.

However, I don't see anything wrong with either parent reminding their children of the day coming up.

It is important, so that the child can see that while mum or dad may not be taking them to buy anything and they may realise that mum or dad do not love each other anymore, at the end of the day their mum is still their mum and their dad is still their dad.

It is very peculiar to a child to spend Father's Day with their mother and her new partner or Mother's Day with their father and his new partner.

Aside from the child feeling strange, the step-parent feels even more strange! And the whole day is a waste because no matter what activities are planned, the elephant in the room is the child not being with the parent for a special day and no one is game to mention it.

Usually this confusion can easily been rectified by simply swapping a weekend. Build a bridge, and realise it is not just one day, but a chance for another block towards building the foundation of a positive future for the children — who may one day may face exactly the same challenges.

To return to the birth of a new baby: there is bound to be a christening or similar occasion.

If it is not possible to swap the weekend to allow your children to attend (assuming they are invited), drop them off on time.

I reiterate the need for flexibility in drop-offs and pick-ups, but when it comes to specific functions you need to pull out all the stops and show your children how to do things the correct way.

Even if you are still angry and jealous — and may well be justified — that is your own anger and jealousy, not your child's. The one thing you can do is spare your children your own hang-ups and insecurities.

As far as they're concerned, it is the christening of their new brother or sister. They probably don't understand the intricacies of the adult dynamics, but they're not going to show you their excitement about the occasion because, chances are, they know how you are feeling.

You may not be able to swap every weekend you like as the other parent is also entitled to arrange things they want to do, but unless it is something crucial just let them go.

Too many parents simply say no because it interrupts their plans.

For the sake of some harmony in these difficult blended family situations, at the end of the day, is it going to muck up your weekend if you just become a little more flexible? Just remember how you would feel if the shoe were on the other foot!

Suggest that if the ceremony is at 2pm, but the party begins at 4pm, they come along to the party or vice versa. Say that it would mean a lot to you if they were able to be a proper part of the celebration, and if it turns out that only one out of the two or three children can come, then so be it.

It is always important to keep those communication lines open between both sides and the new blended family.

I am not saying you need to bend over backwards and gush, but when you drop off your children for a special occasion, simply saying "have a nice time" can and will lift that 10- tonne weight off their already burdened shoulders — and then they will see some normal behaviour which they will remember years down the track.

Sometimes you may have to put your foot down and insist that a child attend a newly blended family occasion, but most of the time the parents should be able to work it out .

Whenever someone separates or divorces, neither person is in the headspace to work out all the alternate weekends and holiday times then and there.

This is uncharted territory for both sides, so why make it even more difficult?

If there are a couple of children, they may have different commitments at the same times. That can't be helped, so don't make a big deal about it. Children do not really want to have to choose what to go to.

Remember, you have a duty to your children.

You made them.

They need to actually see normal behaviour if they are to behave properly as they go through their lives and become parents and step-parents.

As a step-parent, you have to realise that Mother's Day and Father's Day are for them.

Ask your husband whether he would like to spend the day just with his children, or perhaps you can all meet up for lunch or dinner. You need to be flexible with timing as well because they may well run late, but it is just one day and everyone needs to relax and enjoy it.

As much as you may want to do everything with your stepchildren to show them and your partner your commitment, do not forget that they already know that. You are there in their lives, but this is where you can step back a little and show them that you do not feel threatened or left out. A day like Father's Day belongs to them and you can step back.

Everyone needs their own space, and if your partner wants to talk to his children, there are some things he may not be able to say if you are there.

You never know, he may even take the opportunity to ask how they feel about the new situation and remind them that you are doing your best as their stepmother and he hopes that they will always remember that.

At times like these, emotions can run high and things can spring out of nowhere.

On my husband's first Father's Day after his separation, I ordered a cake iced with the children's names. I had not yet met my stepchildren, but I did it as a surprise for him and he really appreciated it.

You might buy your new partner a small gift to acknowledge he is a father — something you would not think of if you have no children. And if his ex will not allow him to be with his children that might cheer him up.

Some stepchildren may love their step-parents more than their real parents, but don't necessarily tell them so.

Some see their stepfather or stepmother as their own parents.

If the relationship is that strong, they could be encouraged to do the same for Mother's or Father's Day as they would for their own parent.

There is no rule book or magic formula. All that is important is respect — and that you feel good about doing something for someone else.

If you are a stepchild and reading this book stop right now! This may be the time to think about your step-parent, who has gone to a lot of trouble over you, and get them something.

Although there is no such thing as Step-Parent Day, there should be! However, in Australia the last Sunday in July is apparently National Stepfamilies Day.

If your step-parent has been a complete nightmare or abused you in any way, you owe them nothing and let the full force of the law be applied.

But perhaps it is time, if you are not doing it already, to show a little appreciation — a text, a card, a call, a gift — whatever you feel is appropriate, but try and do something.

It is unlikely that you will ever know exactly what your step-parents have had to put up with from you and your siblings, or from their partner's ex — who is either your mother or your father.

In my experience step-parents just want to be a positive influence and help you grow into adulthood.

The wars between your parents are really nothing to do with them, but they are caught in the crossfire when it comes to separation and divorce.

They cannot help the fact that they have fallen in love with your parent.

It is time, especially if you are an adult yourself, to realise that this could happen to you. You may well fall in love with someone who is separated or divorced and has children. So let's aim for empathy now and objectivity in seeing your step-parent's role in your life.

If your step-parent does not have any biological children of their own, then you're it!

And nine times out of 10, they are very proud of you and wish that you were their biological child!

I know there are wicked step-parents, just as there are wicked parents, but in the main if you are rowing with your step-parent is it due to a clash of personalities, and frustration over your parents' divorce or separation, or other things going on in your life, and has nothing to do with them.

Imagine having to put up with a stepchild like you every alternate weekend as well as half the school holidays. Could you do it? Would you do it?

Yes, I am flying the flag for the forgotten step-parents of this world, who more often than not end up being the emotional punching bag of their stepchildren and who are fighting the parents' battle because of some perceived sense of loyalty.

All you can ever do is be consistent in your approach, your behaviour and your values, and hope for common sense and respect for someone who is doing their best.

No matter what you believe in, there is a saying that the karma bus comes around at some point and deals to you what you have dealt out to others.

So, best to be good and kind and sleep at night and hold your head high.

It takes more effort to be Machiavellian and deliberately nasty than to just act normally — and we are only human, on the journey of life together with all its ups and downs.

Sometimes we get it right and sometimes we get it wrong, but if we listen and learn we can make a difference in the future. Being able to admit you're wrong is not easy, but an apology speaks volumes both for the person receiving it and for the person making it because it displays a rarely seen maturity.

Chapter Eleven

ALLERGIES, AGONIES AND ALL THAT JAZZ

The new living arrangements will be difficult for everyone. The parents, the children and the step-parents will take time to adjust to shuttling between homes, but it will hit the children the hardest.

However, as the parent, you are responsible for making sure that a Medicare card or a health insurance card, the children's doctor's and dentist's phone numbers and surgery addresses, and any necessary medication the children are at hand.

If the child has allergies — to food, band-aids, toiletries or anything else — then the other parent and new partner need to be aware of them.

You may think this is ridiculous and that the ex must know who the doctor is and what the allergies are, but this is for the child, not you.

Most children live with their mum and their fathers are out at work, so it is their mother who takes them to the doctor or dentist.

It is not as simple as thinking nothing should go wrong between a Thursday night and a Sunday night, because plenty can.

And the children's doctor may not be able to see them and you end up trying to get an appointment with your doctor. Therefore you need their Medicare and Health Insurance cards.

Yes, ringing up or having to go into a Medicare or Health Insurance office is a pain in the neck; no one has time, but your children are your priority, so just get on with getting the second card.

There is also the My Health Update with an Excel document that can be uploaded with all relevant details. But, regardless of whether you are a computer whizz or not, nothing beats a printed out list in a plastic folder, or if you are really schmick, a laminated list.

Nowadays you can check your emails and social media sites as you take a ticket and wait. Just make sure that your children are well covered when they are at the other home.

There is also the vexed question in Australia of whether you are actually covered by bulk billing. Some surgeries do, some surgeries don't.

You may think this is an odd thing to bring up, but, in the case of a parent who pays child support 52 weeks a year, if the child is sick then paying during the weekend for a doctor who does not bulk bill may not be feasible. And if you have not got a second Medicare and/or Health

Insurance card with the various surgery numbers listed it will be even more of a nightmare.

Most parents say they would do anything for their kids, but a man who pays regular child support may live on a very strict budget because there are other obligations as well.

No one is suggesting the child would not be taken to the doctor, but if they are already registered with another doctor who bulk bills and the parent's doctor does not, that unforeseen doctor's bill is another chunk out of an already overstretched budget.

If your child has a bad cold or cough and you cannot keep them with you and swap the designated weekend for a later date, then make sure you send over their cough mixture and any other medication. Do not be the person who sends them with nothing so that at some point during the evening they have to be bundled into the car in their pyjamas to go to a pharmacy.

Time and time again, and despite their family owning pharmacies and their mother working in one, my step-children would arrive on the Thursday night with nothing when they were both clearly unwell. It never ceased to amaze me how they would leave the house coughing and spluttering without even a tissue.

Do not expect the parent whom the children do not normally live with to have a child-stocked medicinal cabinet the whole time.

There was one occasion, before there were 24-hour pharmacies in Melbourne, that I ended up driving across the city to Brunswick at about 11pm one night because the pharmacy there was the only one open until midnight.

All this could have been avoided. Everyone needs to take a deep breath and realise it is the child that suffers. You are doing this for your children. It is also the correct behaviour to demonstrate. The other parent and new partner will be very grateful. And this is all about your children, not about the ex or their new partner.

It shows you are aware of what your children need, and your children see you taking a really active role in their care and responsibility when they are away.

I believe the children's bags should be packed by a parent until they are teenagers and know what to bring and what they need. Until then, have a look at what they pack.

I have outlined the importance of having a working relationship with your ex, even if you are not really on speaking terms. When it comes to your children, you need to put all that bitterness to one side and remember you are talking about the welfare of your children and nothing is more important than that.

If you have a child who suffers from anaphylaxis where expensive EpiPens need to be bought and packed as spares, you must do this.

The price of an EpiPen in Australia has been significantly reduced in recent years as the prevalence of anaphylaxis and awareness of the illness increases. Under Medicare, Australians are able to buy an EpiPen twin-pack for $38 under the Pharmaceutical Benefits Scheme (PBS).

It is a matter of life and death that everyone involved with someone with anaphylaxis not only understand but be able to use an EpiPen correctly.

You must also follow procedure and contact the parent and/or the ex immediately, which is why that mobile must always be on and there should be alternative emergency contact numbers.

That child is the centre of the situation and their welfare is paramount. That must take complete priority over any arguments between the parents and step-parents.

An EpiPen has a shelf life of just under two years, and you may never even need to use one, but, you must remain vigilant, be aware of the expiry date and replace it.

Never say it is a waste if the EpiPen has not been used. An EpiPen is cheaper than a funeral.

There are a myriad of other less serious allergies which need to be taken into account for a step-parent to understand the whole picture.

Children also develop allergies all the time. From hayfever to band-aid rejection. My stepdaughter is allergic to band-aids. Initially, I assumed her mother would tell me what could be used on cuts and grazes instead. I was not going to risk her wrath by trying a new band-aid spray in case that also sparked an allergic reaction.

Aloe vera gel was a good standby.

If your child is going through food fads such as "I don't like peas this week" or "I don't like meat," then let the parent they are going to know.

On the alternate custody weekend, most parents do their best to prepare nice food and if they have made a lasagne for the first night it makes life very difficult to be greeted at the dinner table with "I don't eat meat."

Yes, they could eat toast, but if you had just let your ex know "Johnny is against killing and eating animals this week," then alternative meals could have been made and a battle avoided.

Your job as a parent is 24/7 as well you know, so do not play games with your ex when it comes to your children. It is immature and stupid and, what is worse, you actually know it is and in some cases you could be gambling with their lives.

Take responsibility and manage the situation by being organised, and giving your ex contact details and medications and lists of what has to be done.

They are the child's parent and if you still lived together you would be telling each other. Just because you are separated or divorced does not absolve you of your responsibilities towards your children and your ex.

If you are not on speaking terms, you could use a diary with information about the past week — medications, doctors' appointments.

While you may be angry and aggrieved about having to run around and type up contact details and organise stuff, you will feel better knowing that your children's welfare has been covered to the best of your ability.

Money talks, but I would put together a child's first aid kit of Panadol, antihistamine, cartoon character band-aids, sunscreen and so on. For an initial outlay, it will set the ball rolling and when things need to be replaced, you will probably find they are. And if not, if your ex really is hopeless when it comes to this type of thing, is it really going to break the bank or put you out to do it again?

— Chapter Twelve —

HAIRY BALLS AND THE PERIOD TALK

This is very important.

I think this generation of mothers who perhaps learned about periods and sex from *Dolly* and *Cleo* magazines are far more open when it comes to talking to their daughters about their bodies, sex and periods.

I am not sure how fathers talk to their sons about the changes in their penis size, wet dreams, erections and pubic hair, but the premise is the same.

We have all gone through puberty with its various trials and tribulations, and the one common theme is that so many people wish their parents had explained more to them and been more open instead of their having to discover it all through magazines and schoolyard chit-chat.

Please let your ex know when your daughter has begun menstruation.

There are examples of young girls having had their periods for at least six months and the other parent and/ or partner having no idea.

It is pure chance if the young girl does not get her period when she is staying with the other parent.

Neither parent should make a big deal about it, but at least they can make sure they have a packet of sanitary pads or tampons in the bathroom drawer.

Even if you do not want to speak to your ex, you can send an email or text along the lines of "please don't make a big deal about it, but our daughter has begun her period, I will try and make sure she always has something in her bag, but could you make sure you have something at your place too just in case?"

Do not behave in a mean or immature way if your ex has remarried and assume the stepmother will have something and know what to do. Perhaps the stepmother no longer has a period or perhaps she uses sanitary pads but your daughter wants to use tampons, or vice-versa.

It is up to you to think ahead. What if your daughter gets her period while she is there and is embarrassed? And, if you are her mother, talk to your daughter about periods, hygiene during menstruation and what to do with the used pads or tampons.

In an ideal world, if the mother is on the scene, the stepmother (girl to girl is a lot easier — no offence to all the single dads out there who are doing a terrific job) does not want to be the one to have to give the period talk to their stepdaughter. If the period suddenly arrives when she is staying then of course she will, but she would primarily see it as the mother's role and think she was overstepping the mark by doing so.

So if you have a daughter and have not thought about this yet, please do. Some girls begin at nine or 10, some earlier and others anywhere between 11 and 17.

It is your responsibility as a mother and as a woman to make things as smooth as possible.

It is about not involving the stepmother who really does not want to be embroiled in something as personal as this.

Just notify your ex. You owe it to your daughter and you owe it to your ex. Once upon a time you would have been discussing this face to face. Your situation has changed, but you are the parents of a young daughter who is entering a new phase of life. It is not right to hide your head in the sand.

It is also not right to assume that boys do not need some attention and understanding when it comes to puberty.

I think we are all guilty of thinking that they'll be right, or that their dad will sort it out, but many men have never had puberty explained to them.

Schools do their best with sex education, but the giggles and confusion of a classroom mean that questions the students are perhaps too embarrassed to ask (as we all remember when we were their age) need to be addressed at home.

This generation is far more open about sex education and puberty. For my generation it wasn't that it was a taboo subject, but some people had sex education and a lot of people didn't.

My stepson was lucky in that my husband was there and very happy to answer his questions.

I was relieved that this was the case. It is difficult for any adult to have these conversations with children.

Some fathers say that because no one really explained to them they hope their children's mother and the stepmother can simply work it out.

This head in the sand, 'she'll be right' approach just adds to the confusing complexities of the situation.

From a stepmother's point of view, we hope that you and your ex will have sorted out who, when, where and how it will be discussed

The step-parent wants to be in the background and only be involved if there really is no other option.

All I did was to remind my stepson of the importance of becoming a young man and say that young men sweat and need to shower and wash more, including under there!

There was always plenty of shampoo, conditioner, shower gels and toiletries. A toothbrush and toothpaste set was kept separately too.

There were always half-a-dozen pairs of socks, sports socks and jocks at our house and the importance of changing every day or even twice a day if going out was emphasised.

It did not mean that actually happened as teenagers will always be teenagers!

When my stepson began shaving, I gave him a few tips such as not using his body towel on his face when the pores were open as that can cause infection, so to use a separate smaller towel. Making sure his shaving brush was washed thoroughly as you would remind girls to wash their makeup brushes, and to refrain from squeezing any spots or pimples as that would lead to infection and make acne or skin conditions worse. Checking that his razor blade was sharp and making sure he used hot water and had clean hands.

Incredibly straightforward, conversational things, most of which he already knew but, since he trusted me and I wasn't his mum or dad, he listened!

It is difficult to believe at the time, but when laying the foundations for a more harmonious working relationship within the stepfamily dynamic, things do get noticed.

Years later, I told my stepson that even though I had known him since he was 12 and was trying to see him as a 25-year-old man and to give him the respect due to an adult, I would always give him tips.

I thanked him again for always acknowledging me on special occasions. Now we live interstate, a phone call or a text means even more.

At the time he said "that's no worries."

The next day, he actually texted me and said " Thanks, KT, for always being so kind to me as well. It's my pleasure to text you on those occasions. I want you to know that I see all you do, and you might think you just do it, but what you do is truly fantastic. Most other people wouldn't have a single idea what to do or how to do it. You always keep the show on the road. (other banter) signed Lots of love xxx".

This message signed "lots of love' showed me that 14 years of hard yards had paid off. (by the way, it hadn't taken him 14 years to say, 'I love you' but you get the general idea of how being the best I could be and demonstrating, being consistent, not playing games always pays off.)

That does not mean I was waiting for a text signed "lots of love", but it meant that my approach had worked. I had not played any games or entered into any bitterness between his mum and dad, and had just focused on what I could do, what I would do and how I could behave to achieve a better outcome each time.

Step-parenting does not get fixed overnight. But if you put in the effort — and with the tips and examples I give throughout this book I hope you are getting a clearer picture of how things can be turned around and how they can be — you can prevail.

– Chapter Thirteen –

THE ROLE OF THE CHILDREN

I use the term children for any biological offspring be they two years old or 30.

From my own research, it does not seem to matter what age a child is when their parents separate or divorce, they all deal with it in different ways.

One of the saddest stories I keep hearing is of people who have stayed together for the sake of the children and divorced when their children hit their twenties. Then the grown-up children behave immaturely and make it all about them, instead of looking at their parents' relationship as adults.

Whether they want to admit it or not, children know when things are not right at home over the years.

People don't separate on a whim or overnight; it is something that has been building up over a long period of time.

People often feel that it is never the right time to split, and when the couple does friends and family react with surprise.

The bottom line is that if the decision has been made, it has been made. If a couple do not want to remain together everyone must respect that decision. It does not matter why; what does matter is that a decision has been made by these two adults.

One very sad situation where the adult children acted more like juveniles when they should have known better was when a couple divorced after 35 years of marriage. They had simply grown apart.

Their children were aged 34, 33 and 31.

The man went on to marry a close family friend who had divorced more than a decade earlier, and she also had three children aged 26, 24, 22.

The two couples had moved in the same social circles and knew each other. Their children all got on extremely well with one another.

But once the man married again, his children in their 30s would not visit him, citing loyalty to their mother and continually telling him he had broken up the family.

When the woman's daughter got married she invited her new stepfather to the celebrations, but a week later when his daughter got married, she did not invite her new stepmother.

You cannot begin to know how you will act or feel until you have walked a day in someone else's shoes.

This woman's parents sacrificed their own happiness for a couple of decades until they felt their own children had finished studying, begun new jobs, settled down, etc.

The daughter has a right to be angry about the breakdown of her family unit, but this is immature behaviour. She is in her 30s and married with her own family, which should be her number one priority. Naturally we all want our parents to be happy, but life moves on and you have to live in the present.

For anyone in their 20s, 30s or even 40s whose parents are separated or divorced, you know that this is just one of those things.

Yes, you may be angry if one of your parents has an affair, but do not take it out on your step-parent, even if they are the so-called guilty party.

You have no way of knowing what actually happened.

You may not like to think so, but your father or mother may have told their new partner that they were already separated, even if technically they weren't at the time.

Maybe they did have an affair.

They may be your mother or father but, whether you want to read this or not, at the end of the day it is not any of your business.

This is a very confronting thing to read, but life is not a dress rehearsal. Marriage is a lottery. Some people win straightaway; others may need a second chance when the time is right. One of the most important things for every human being is to be happy and loved.

Some got married too young or felt pressured due to a situation. Some did not grow together in the marriage, but grew apart. No one knows how a marriage will turn out.

And no one walks down the aisle not expecting to live happily ever after.

So whether your mum and dad are young or old, if they believe they have found this opportunity again, you just have to support them as I am sure they have supported you all your life.

Even when you did or pursued something your parents were not too happy about, chances are they stood by you because you were their child.

As a fully grown adult, you need to take a proper look at your parents. We all want to think of our parents as just our mum and dad and forget that other people see them as adults. Because of our relationship with them we do not. No one ever wants to think of their parents having sex, but they do or we wouldn't even be here! And you never want to think that your children will have sex, but they will otherwise you wouldn't be a grandparent!

We are not talking about the mum or dad in the nursing home where a blatant gold digger 30 years their junior is making romantic moves and trying to get them to change their will.

If that is the case, you have every right to react when those alarm bells start ringing.

What we are talking about is the traditional breakdown of a couple and how people do move on whether we like it or not.

You do not have to like your new step-parent, but for the sake of your biological parent make an effort.

Life's ironies happen when you least expect them and you can bet your bottom dollar that one day it will be your step-parent who physically steps up to the plate to help you out either as an adult or a new parent.

If you have spent years treating them like rubbish your conscience may kick in, but by then it will be too late.

In the case I outlined earlier where the stepdaughter would not invite her stepmother to the wedding or even speak to her, she ended up needing her stepmother after she had given birth and was suffering from post-natal depression. Her own mother was more worried about the social stigma of her daughter suffering what she thought only happened to Hollywood or reality TV stars.

The stepmother just rolled up her sleeves and provided practical help such as looking after the baby, driving her stepdaughter to medical appointments, cooking meals, and doing the washing and ironing.

Once the post-natal depression had passed, the stepdaughter was filled with guilt as she really did realise what her stepmother had done that own mother could not.

The stepmother was a practical woman and all was forgiven. Their relationship found new ground, but it was hard work all the way.

Being a step-parent really is a thankless task at times. You cop a lot of rubbish and always have to be the one to rise above stuff otherwise you end up looking like the villain.

You need as much support as possible. If you have not

supported your own parent, can you count on support yourself?

In an ideal world no one would break up, no one would have affairs, no one would argue. But none of us lives in an ideal world. You cannot guarantee you won't have an affair just as you cannot guarantee that your partner won't.

How will you feel about your parent or step-parent, when you tread the same path?

No one has the perfect solution to every problem or situation in life. We just have to hope that given enough experience we will choose the right way to handle things.

As I said earlier, it is not the set of cards you are dealt in life, but rather how you deal with that set of cards in each situation.

It is very difficult when anyone's parents separate or divorce, but the end of an era is not the end of the world. It is a new start and it is up to you how you behave.

You do not have to suddenly become best buddies with your new step-parent — just extend normal courtesy as to a new work colleague.

You may have your reservations about the person and that is completely normal, but you have to work with this new person in your life.

Whether you end up seeing them once a week, once a month or once a year, the chances are you will have to see them and you need to look at this step-parent as a person, not as a person with horns on their head.

Your new step-parent is evidently someone very special to your parent, and the dynamics of family life have now changed forever.

There is no point worrying about the hypothetical Christmases, or weddings down the track and how you will seat people. Just deal with the here and now.

Control what you think, say, look and act.

Your step-parent is not going to be on your other parent's Christmas card list, but there is no reason, unless they have treated you dreadfully, why they should not be on yours.

When my friends knew I was writing this book, they sent examples of what had happened to them and their friends.

A lot of the time it was simply a chance to get things that had been bottled up for years off their chests. If I was that outlet I'm pleased, but there were too many stories to include, although there was an all too often a similar thread transcending any socioeconomic factors.

Instead, that thread boiled down to the whole step-parenting, blended family, 'love happening a second time around' dynamic combined with the continual underlying tension that happens all too often in these situations.

One story was about a man who was married for 25 years and had two sons and two daughters, all of whom are married with small children, but only one of his sons still sees him.

He and his first wife had met in their early twenties.

She had raised their four children with the help of a live-in nanny. There had been private schooling, overseas holidays and an incredibly high standard of living.

The reason for the separation was not the second wife. It was a classic example of two people meeting fairly young and then simply growing apart. This can happen at any age.

He once went with his middle-aged girlfriend, now his second wife, to an exhibition and his eldest son actually spat at her.

The eldest son's mother had a new partner, but that meant nothing to him. For years the mother's new partner still had to put up with her continual "I can't believe he left me and his four children for that woman and her son," and he did.

This eldest son is entitled to his anger, but more often than not history repeats itself in families and I wonder how he will feel if he finds himself in his father's shoes 20 years from now.

Will how he behaved come flooding back to him when his father is dead, or too old for the relationship to be repaired?

If his father wanted to see his grandchildren he had to go over to his children's houses to meet them on his own, a huge price to pay for a devoted family man.

The stepmother had been a single mother in her 50s who had worked for his father briefly. Two mature, middle-aged adults made this decision. The son would probably have behaved in the same way towards any other woman in his father's life.

A lot of stress was put on the younger son who remained in contact with the new wife. While his sisters may have admired him for doing so when they did not have the strength to rise above their hurt feelings, he was made to feel very uncomfortable.

He never gossiped to score points. He simply wanted to see both parents happy again. Naturally, he would have preferred his mother and father remain together, but he was able to see their marriage really had been drifting for many years and he figured that his father's new wife was doing her best.

The grandchildren's first birthdays were held at the multimillion-dollar family home and the grandfather was invited — alone, of course, but it was like the elephant in the room. All the guests could sense the tension and knew the whole situation, and the first wife's new partner was always invited which seemed to be fine with all the adult children.

It was a big price to pay. He had minimal contact with three of his four children and only really saw two of his six grandchildren.

To an outsider looking in, he seemed to have given up all this for a single mother of a seven-year-old, but in the end love conquers all.

I took my hat off to him because he had made the decision rather than stay in a marriage for the sake of keeping up appearances. He had followed his heart.

He and his second wife married overseas without telling anyone, not even the son he was in daily contact with so that when all the siblings found out they could not accuse their brother of knowing or even being the best man.

His mother's annoyance that he was in contact with his father showed when his children were the only ones she would never babysit.

I once watched an interview with Denise Richards after her well documented divorce from Charlie Sheen. She was alleged to have had an affair with Richie Sambora, the ex-husband of Heather Locklear.

Denise Richards stopped the reporter in her tracks when she said "Seriously, how can someone actually steal a husband away? It's not as if you have shackles and chains, now is it?!"

I have always remembered that "she stole my husband" was the default position in this example, and no doubt of many men and women and indeed men who cannot see they have done anything wrong.

It takes two to tango.

Not all marriages that have lasted 50 years are golden. Marriages depend on when you meet someone.

As they get older, most people say that they are not the same person at 25 that they were at 17, and at 30 they are not the same person they were at 25.

The essence of your values and personality are no

doubt the same, but your life goals and dreams may have changed depending on your life.

More people are getting married later in life and come to their relationships with more idea of what they want and are looking for. They may also be more set in their ways, and then have to learn how to compromise.

It is a double-edged sword.

You cannot put an old head on young shoulders, but as long as you learn from experience you will grow and become a better person.

We all know in a break-up there are what I call a 'dumper' and a 'dumpee'.

It is much easier for the dumper than for the dumpee, because when someone has decided they want out of a relationship they are in a completely different mindset.

Very few relationships end at exactly the same time with both people deciding together, but break-ups are a fact of life. There is a time for the tears, the anger, the upset, the hurt — but then, most importantly, for moving on.

That does not mean jumping straight into a new relationship. If you do that you will not be much good to the new person, let alone yourself.

People often say that human beings are not meant to be alone, that we are meant to be paired up, but I argue someone should be comfortable in their own skin and know themselves before they meet someone new.

Some people are relieved when a relationship ends as

it means they have time to find themselves again and can to do what they want without constraints.

That does not mean you go and have a whole series of one-night stands to try and find your self-worth. You should know your self-worth already.

It means being able to go out to the movies with friends, have dinner, exercise or just stay in pyjamas on a Friday or Saturday night in front of the TV with a take-away and a tub of ice-cream.

Not spending any time by yourself and simply hooking up with someone to take away the loneliness will not do you any good in the long run.

Someone else on the rebound will probably not make you happy.

Only you can make yourself happy, and once you find that inner happiness it will radiate and attract whatever you want to attract.

You will never forget your separation or divorce, but life moves on and you can move on and begin living the best way you can.

If someone does not want to be with you anymore, that is a sad fact you have to accept.

You can lock yourself in your house for the next 20 years or you can get professional help and realise that life is still out there, but you must learn to accept reality.

These are uncharted waters for your teenage stepchild too. A time to compare and contrast what their step-parent does and what their parent does not.

You will have a chance to score points.

Firm but fair is the key, and you can explain that this whole step-parenting thing is new to you and you are not prepared to get caught in the middle of anything. And that if you know their mother or father does not want them to go to a party on their weekend with you, you won't let them go either to score points or so they think you're cool.

They will probably respect you more if you make light of it and say you are just their stepmother and they have to work it out with their mum or dad.

That firm but fair approach will show them that you are not a pushover and that you do respect their mum and dad.

You just have to grin and bear those teenage years — there is light at the end of the tunnel!

Yes, your stepchildren will be a complete nightmare at times, yet remarkable little angels at others. They will be as nice as pie to you when they want you to let them do something and then unbearable when they do not get their own way.

History shows that the years pass and most things will be forgotten.

We have all been teenagers with ratty, petulant moods and those hormones running riot, harming whoever happens to be in the vicinity with our tongue-lashing, but we all recover.

For those under 12 it is simple. As I say in this book, they will be continually brainwashed and if you have them on alternate weekends a couple of nights every two weeks is not enough to undo that.

All I can recommend is to let your actions speak for themselves, and in time those children will notice that you do not bad-mouth their mum or dad.

It may well take a few years, but you will eventually be streets ahead of their own parents if you follow some of my advice.

Just remember, it is normal and understandable if you are living a step-parenting hell on earth to be fed up with the stepchildren who are encroaching on your life.

Perhaps write a journal and let your feelings out in that?

Or just take a deep breath, but never ever tell them — or even your new partner as they are their children — and how would you feel if the situation were reversed?

One exception to this rule: if your stepchild assaults you physically or verbally, swears at you or destroys your property when your partner is not around, then you have to say something. But this is the extreme.

There isn't a step-parent around though who has not wished at some time they could have a break from all the drama that surrounds separation and divorce!

They could not help whom they fell in love with, but their stepchildren did not ask for their world to be changed either.

It is all about being willing to compromise as well as negotiate.

Children will be children — and there is a child in all of us.

We all wish life was simpler at times — and hindsight is a marvellous thing. If hindsight could magically become the here and now, we would be excellent masters of our own destinies!

— Chapter Fourteen —

SCHOOL

Children have enough to deal with at school.

Throw a separation or divorce into the mix and what were a few molehills can very easily become mountains.

It is normal for parents to go to parent-teacher interviews, but what if one parent cannot make an interview?

Lives are very busy and evening work commitments are common. Traffic snarls in busy metropolitan cities and it's common to sit still on a freeway. Is a call to the partner saying you are not going to be able to make the parent-teacher interview and could they go instead really outside the realm of possibilities?

In some situations, absolutely!

But if one parent cannot make the interview and the other parent, with the best of intentions, is in a traffic jam, isn't it better that an adult with the child's best interests at heart go?

There may not be grandparents available, and the step-parent may be ready, willing and able to step up, but not allowed to due the sheer pig-headedness of one parent .

STEP-PARENTING WITH PURPOSE

Step-parents want to be involved in their stepchildren's lives, but must be very careful not to overstep the mark even if they know how to keep their distance.

Should they be allowed to go or not?

A parent may feel that a poor report card could be used by the step-parent to try and gain the upper hand, but this book is all about showing children that they are the important ones in all this.

They might like mum or dad's new partner coming to their school and finding out what is going on there.

If the kids have continually been playing mum and dad off against each other, just knowing that a step-parent will be at their parent-teacher interview may be all that is needed to stop some spoilt behaviour.

Children often feel upset in what we as adults regard as pretty standard situations, so they could feel equally strange if only one parent were there or if a step-parent were there.

But regardless of what feels more strange, the child knows that someone cares enough go and see their teacher. Things do not have to be turned into a battle or a game of one-upmanship, and need not be that way at all.

Keep the lines of communication open and life becomes easier for everyone.

The fight to keep your old relationship has already been lost and you cannot keep trying to have the last word through spite.

What happens at end-of-term concerts, recitals and graduations?

If there are only two tickets issued, that question is easily answered, but what if the children are asked to bring their family? What does that mean to them?

Can their mum and dad sit with their new partners in the same row while they sing carols, dance their routines, play their instruments or recite their verses?

It all boils down to keeping those lines of communication open!

It is the same with school camps.

Some private schools do a term at a country campus or town designed to instil more independence into children and show them another way of life.

When parents wave them goodbye for eight weeks it is a big milestone in their child's life.

Yes, most children are embarrassed by mum and dad being there as they pile into the bus, but they feel weird anyway. We have all been in that situation.

And they surely feel even worse knowing their step-parent could not come and wave them off because one of their parents would object, so more often than not the step-parent has had to say goodbye on the last visit or the night before they leave.

You should be pleased by the very fact that a step-parent would want to support your child by waving them off and wishing them a safe journey. They are involved in the upbringing of your child. And are you really so insecure that you worry your child may forget you and shower the step-parent with more attention?

The upset resulting from a separation or divorce will always be there, but that is just one of those things. Children do learn to adapt.

Things will never be the same for them, but life will never be the same for you either. We all want things to turn out perfectly, but, sadly, often life does not work like that.

Recognise that while your ex's new partner may be your least favourite person in the world and you wish they would simply disappear, there is a strong possibility that your children like or even love their mum or dad's new partner.

You need to understand that is their relationship, not yours, and the sooner you do, the easier it will be.

This is not a competition for whom your child loves more. It never was and it never should be.

Your children will always have an innate loyalty to you, always, even if you are a dreadful parent. But they should not have to choose between you and their step-parent on every occasion for the rest of their lives.

If they do, they will probably end up moving interstate or overseas to make their life easier so they no longer have to continually juggle holidays and birthdays.

You may think you are the most accommodating person in the world, but look at the situation through your child's eyes.

Admit that it is possible to have a very happy life second time around, and take the chance to show your children that, should this ever happen to them, they can rise above the bitterness and anger. Demonstrate through your own behaviour that by keeping those lines of communication open we can all help raise a future generation of grounded stepchildren, step-parents and parents who will thank us for it.

– Chapter Fifteen –

IT'S A MAN'S WORLD

My husband and I have a funny term for when we relay stories or events to each other.

He says "Do you want the Peter version or the KT version?" (My maiden name was Karalee Tilvern, hence KT, and my stepchildren refer to me as KT).

What he essentially means is do you want the short, sharp to the point summary (the Peter version) or the more in-depth, feeling, elaborate story (the KT version).

As the years roll by, he realises it is a man/woman thing, but he has come to appreciate the value of the KT version.

Peter says that as a divorced man with two children, having been able to observe what I have been through allows him credibility to raise certain points.

So, I give you Chapter Fifteen.

Again, I do not profess to have the foolproof formula to help you in every situation, but hopefully you will be able to take away some ideas, strategies and insights to keep you on the right path.

When it comes to separation or divorce, it is not really a man's world.

No matter how it happens, whether it is one person or both, an affair or simply growing apart, cultural differences, addictions or domestic violence, it is tough.

A man loses the 24/7 access to his children and is usually relegated to the alternate weekend, which hurts. His world has fallen apart and he may feel guilty.

You may even separate and then get back together a few times before breaking up for good, all in the desperate hope that things will change or the person will change.

The truth is, the world as you have known it in recent years has actually fallen apart. That is what separation and divorce does. There is no such thing as a happy divorce. There is always pain on every level.

However, some couples are more mature and recognise their union does not work any more, and that while they do not hate each other, they both deserve to find happiness with someone else or just be happy by themselves rather than spend even more time in a loveless, difficult marriage.

You are essentially grieving for the dream you set out on when you walked down the aisle, which never actually came to fruition. And, for better or worse, now is not the time to point the finger of blame. Sometimes things just do not work out the way you envisaged.

There are stages that you have to work through —a series of one night stands is not the answer. That leaves a trail of even more destruction in your wake as you get angrier and angrier at yourself.

Some people work through these stages quicker than others; some never do and become stuck in a bitter no-man's land.

What you have to realise is that although your world has now changed forever, it really is possible to move on, fall in love again if you want to, and maintain a relationship with your children.

It is not the end of the world, only the end of the world as you have known it since your children were born.

In Australia, the media always seizes on the rare fathers who kill their children due to bitter custody battles, and while it is more common for men to abuse their children and stepchildren, it does not mean that all men do or that all men are monsters.

Such men are undoubtedly tortured individuals, and although at times, perhaps due to media coverage, it seems that more people are doing this, it is rare. Most men want to achieve success in an uphill battle by working out the best way to separate and support their children.

One example of an uphill battle that springs to mind is a Queensland family court ruling that four daughters must return to Italy to live with their father.

The girls' great-grandmother took them into hiding. They confronted the High Court and were allowed to stay in Australia until another hearing in August 2012.

When my husband and I watched this, he said if the

court ruled the girls were to live with their mother, and the father's grandmother took them into hiding, the father would be held in contempt of court and jailed.

And he was absolutely right.

In 2012, when Australia passed legislation that parents would get an educational bonus of $400 for primary schoolchildren and $800 for secondary schoolchildren, a friend who was divorced with a teenage daughter said "I pay my child support, yet this is going to the mother. Where is the fairness in that? Should it not be divided between the parents?"

I have already said that Child Support Payments are the bane of everyone's lives because they are so regimented, and more often than not when a mother rings up the CSA whatever she says about her ex is taken as gospel so, instead of the CSA ringing up to check, a letter goes out and it is up to the ex to prove otherwise.

Perhaps CSA officers need training to work out that if a divorce or financial settlement is going through or the client is in the initial stages of separation and emotions are running high, ludicrous claims are often made to spite the other person.

Next time a man rings the Child Support Agency, remember that as stressful as your job is, you have an real person, often a man, calling who is living with their stress 24/7.

Please stop reading from a script and do not automatically assume that he is a bad person. He is ringing to ask something. For every man who trying to avoid paying child support, there are many more busting their butt to do the right thing. All the bloke wants to do is talk to a human being to try and solve his problem.

Most divorced men I know do not mind supporting their children from previous relationships, but they do mind having no control over how and where the money is spent — and whether it is actually spent on their children.

Nothing infuriates a man more than another man living in the house and off their hard-earned money, which should be spent on their children, not utility bills, rent or the mortgage.

Child Support is a huge millstone, but it is necessary, although it is apparent that no one in a government department ever shops on special, looks at the weekly store special catalogues or walks from a K-Mart to a Big W or Target to compare prices.

When you have children you shop around for the best prices.

Insurance companies always remind people never to underinsure their possessions, but retail prices are very different to what you paid in the New Year sales, so you would need to claim about double what you actually paid.

Thus the Child Support Amount, which increases when a child turns 13, often seems out of step. Child Support is separate from parents' previous obligations.

Around 35 per cent of Australian children attend private schools. School fees are a very big responsibility.

And it seems unfair that, regardless of whether you have children for half or the whole holidays, the child support payment remains the same.

Having children for four weeks and paying for food, outings, airfares, etc., as well as paying full child support puts an enormous strain on a budget.

No man should make the classic mistake and say "She is the mother of my children and I am going to sign everything over to her." Noble thoughts from a good place, which may later prove incredibly damaging, because if you got married at 25 and are at 40 in the throes of a divorce, you cannot get back the last 15 years' earnings.

And as a woman, if you got married at 23, had two children and some time off work, and are now working part-time, your earnings have already been reduced and it's going to be even harder to take on a full-time job with sole parenting responsibilities at set times.

You are nearer to retirement at 40 than you were at 25, and you have to factor that in.

Some couples divorce amicably, but emotions tend to run high and you probably need objective professional advice. You cannot afford not to have a lawyer to look after your interests. Representing yourself in court usually ends up as a bumbling, emotional mess with everyone flustered and upset.

You need what you are entitled to and if you do the settlement yourself you will get duded. Either you or your ex will meet someone else, and have to begin all over again.

It is not as simple as getting a one-bedroom flat, eating takeaways every night, watching as much TV as you want to without being nagged, and saying "She'll be right, mate."

Because she won't be right, mate.

Whether you have one child or more ,you need somewhere they can stay. You need to furnish it and buy bedding, and that costs money. Life changes to a completely different dynamic.

If you have signed everything over, no matter how lovely your ex is or has been, where does that leave you? Love may make the world go round, but it doesn't pay the bills.

And if you have signed everything over with the best of intentions because she is the mother of your children, it limits your future.

How many times do couples split up with no third party in the picture and swear never to get married or involved with anyone again, only to find themselves absorbed in a new relationship?

Men are territorial, and if you know another man is sleeping with your ex and living in the same house as your kids while you are struggling in a bedsit, you're likely to see red and not be as generous.

If you sign over everything blindly and do not get proper legal advice, your future is limited. If you meet another woman and you have absolutely nothing, how are you going to build a life together?

At least if you have received a fair financial settlement, you will have some equity to be able to buy a place together, although you will still have to foot the bills for school, sporting activities, school camps, birthday parties, holidays, child support, etc.

There was a time where my husband was paying out so much he was left with literally $20 in his wallet every fortnight. No wonder so many men commit suicide, turn to alcohol or give up on life and become homeless.

Many people often think of the stereotypical image that homeless men have just gambled and drunk their lives away which is why they find themselves in the predicament they are. However, so many I have met all of whom had started out with the very best of intentions, giving everything to their ex, but forgetting that they were worthy people too.

You cannot apportion blame to just one side — but both parties are entitled to move on with dignity.

Be reasonable and make it a fair settlement — which the courts will more often than not decide anyway.

A summary — Learning to lead your life again

While your children are the most important thing in your life, and so they should be, they will grow up and leave the nest. But your children should not be your whole life.

You are an individual who has the right to meet someone else and to move forward with them.

Whether that is a Brady Bunch life, a life with no more

children or a life with more children, apart from your responsibilities, you should not feel guilty if your marriage has not worked out. Marriage is a lottery.

Sometimes it works, sometimes it does not. People change, sometimes for the better, sometimes for the worse.

Sometimes the person you married at 25 is a different person at 35.

Be aware of rebound relationships. It is natural to be flattered after being rejected, but no one wants to be told that they are on the rebound — or that they are the rebound.

By the time the separation or divorce actually comes off, the couple will have had their problems for more years than they care to be reminded of.

In other words, do not start something — you do not know where it will go.

However, when it actually comes to signing your divorce papers, more often than not there is a hesitation and many men, despite having embarked headlong on a fully-fledged relationship with someone else, end up hurting yet another person when they go back to their wife.

We all know the cliché "he went back to his wife". Many couples choose to live separate lives under the same roof for the sake of the children and because of what they stand to lose financially.

Some men, and indeed some women, will actually

wait until their children have turned 18 and left school to initiate divorce proceedings, because they will not have to pay child support.

And while child support is a necessary thing, there is a jungle of bureaucratic red tape that many men become mired in, from the endless on hold as they try to get a simple question answered to the built-in prejudice of most female Child Support Agency workers when a man calls, although a mother ringing up can claim anything and her word is more often than not simply taken as gospel.

Common sense from agency workers would go a long way in improving the reputation of the CSA.

Being a single parent is tough, but men who do not lodge tax returns in order to avoid paying child support or who fiddle their income have carved out a rough path for the majority who are responsible, loving fathers.

So, no wonder there are men who see the system as flawed.

From what I have seen, Many men do indeed get the rough end of the deal and so cannot help but see the current CSA system as flawed.

I myself have heard the tone of voice on the phone to the CSA and the male staff members are definitely more sympathetic to the male caller than their female colleagues.

While children love to have the latest toy or gadget, in years to come, they will remember the things you have done with them and you saying that you love them.

Reminding them that even though you may not love their mother any more, you still love them is so important.

Your primary job as a father is to love your children.

The rest will happen.

If you have had a tempestuous relationship with your ex, your children will know.

Children are very perceptive and staying together for the sake of the kids is really not the thing to do.

A happy home free from conflict is needed, and if that happy home ends up being spread over two homes, then so be it.

Do not fall into the trap of being the good time dad who does things simply because he knows his ex won't, like having treats in the pantry that their mother never allowed.

Do not worry about being strict and putting your foot down. Many men fear that if they raise their voice their children will not want to visit them again. Nothing could be further from the truth.

The children usually look forward to seeing their father, relieved to get away from the mother who disciplines them, and are on cloud nine, counting the days until they come over.

If your children turn up with no clothes or shoes one weekend or shoes, do not go out on a buying spree for them.

Do not fall into the trap, that so many Dads do, because it is indeed just that, a trap.

If you have family functions to attend, as embarrassing as it will be, be strong and take them in the clothes that are packed in their bags.

If people ask why they are in their school uniform, or old clothes, have the guts to say "Well, unfortunately this was all their mother packed for them."

You may think this is all very well on paper, but what if it is someone's wedding and they have nothing to wear?

This is where the flexibility that I talk about throughout this book comes into play.

If you have genuinely forgotten to pack your children's dressy clothes, let them fetch them while the other parent waits in the car.

We are all human, and all guilty of forgetting things.

But if you capitulate and go and buy a whole new outfit, chances are — and history shows — that you will never see it again.

The pattern will be repeated regularly: your children will arrive without clothes or shoes because your ex realises her emotional blackmail is working. She would not think in a million years that you would dare take them to the function in the school uniform or old clothes, and this is exactly what she is banking on. The fact that she knows you would not take them anywhere dressed in what she has put in their bags. No matter how tempting it is, resist.

Parents can be incredibly smart about playing games like this, but if they see you have not fallen for it, they'll stop bothering.

They will be mortified that you actually took the children out in the school uniform they arrived in at your house or wore the inappropriate clothes they had packed.

They will go into complete panic mode thinking everyone in your family, of which they were once a part, now believes that they are a complete piece of work. They may yell and swear at you. But it will never ever happen again.

They took you to the brink and you did not flinch. Remember that.

The reason why they played these games in the first place was to see exactly what you would do. And most men worry about what people would think if they took their children in inappropriate clothes — and their instinct is to protect the mother of their children even though the union is no more.

The mother knows, or at least thinks she knows, that the ex-husband will still protect her name and image, but there are limits.

If the children are young, you may well have to buy a set of pyjamas and underwear, toothbrushes and toiletries to keep at your house. But do not fall into the trap of double buying everything. You pay child support.

The child support is for your child or children to be fed and clothed by the primary carer parent.

It took more than two years for my husband's ex-wife to drop off or pick up the children. Her attitude was "he divorced me; if he wants to see his kids then he has to come and get them and bring them back."

She behaved exactly like her new partner's ex-wife — a classic case of the pot calling the kettle black!

It takes a very strong person to admit they have been in the wrong.

Past behaviour is a strong indicator of future behaviour.

However, acknowledgement that someone has been behaving badly because they were hurt would go a long way.

"Happy wife, happy life" is not applicable when you are separating.

Your wife will never really be happy that about it unless she initiated it.

Even if you have had an affair, there will be a part of her that wants you back in the desperate hope she can change you.

The fact of the matter is that if you have had an affair, you had it for a reason.

No matter what the reason is, it happened. You cannot change what happened, but you can analyse why it happened.

Sometimes men, and indeed women, have affairs because they actually want to get found out so they can leave.

None of us live in an ideal world. Affairs do happen and have happened since the dawn of time.

You cannot stop people falling in and out of love, but you can stop for a moment and look into the future to make sure that you have one.

It is possible to have a very happy life the second time around, and you can show your children how to rise above bitterness and anger and, by keeping those lines of communication open, raise future generations who will thank you.

Being a step-parent is not easy. It takes time and dedication, and at times you will be tempted to put it all in the too-hard basket. But it is worth it and I hope this book reaffirms this.

"A stepparent doesn't just marry a spouse: they marry their spouse's entire situation. They have to find a balance between supporting and defending without overstepping visible and invisible boundaries."- Pinterest

EPILOGUE

I thank you for reading this book.

At the very beginning, I posed three questions:

Do you wish there was a step-parent handbook full of advice that actually works?

Do you want a really happy stepfamily?

Do you want someone to help you navigate the challenging situation of step-parenting?

I hope the answer to all these questions was yes and that this book now helps you to be an effective step-parent.

I hope that these 15 chapters will help revolutionise or at least reaffirm your life as a step-parent, knowing you are not alone!

I remain committed to doing the best job I can as a step-parent.

This is my story, this is my life. I hope it helps you in your journey too.

For more information or to contact Karalee please
go to **www.karaleekatsambanis.com**

To purchase books go to:
www.karaleekatsambanis.com

Follow Karalee's Blog here:
www.karaleekatsambanis.com/blog

To contact Karalee for speaking
and media engagements
please contact her at
karaleekatsambanis1@gmail.com